Economic Progress and Prospects
in the Third World

Economic Progress and Prospects in the Third World

Lessons of Development Experience Since 1945

H.W. Singer and Sumit Roy

The Institute of Development Studies
at the University of Sussex
Brighton, UK

Edward Elgar

Published by
Edward Elgar Publishing Limited
Gower House
Croft Road
Aldershot
Hants GU11 3HR
England

Edward Elgar Publishing Company
Old Post Road
Brookfield
Vermont 05036
USA

A CIP catalogue record for this book is available from the British Library

A CIP catalogue record for this book is available from US Library of Congress

Printed in Great Britain at the University Press, Cambridge

ISBN 1 85278 649 3

Contents

PART 3   THE 1990s

Tables

Preface

Millions of people in the Third World live in abject poverty and turmoil emanating from disruptions to the global and the domestic economy. A combination of rising debts, unemployment, starvation and environmental degradation confront many developing countries in Africa, Asia and Latin America. Thus, how to bring about sustainable growth and to eradicate poverty forms the main focus of current and future development policies. This demands forceful policies on both the global and the domestic front.

This book aims to capture the major shifts and changes in development thinking and development strategy over the last almost fifty years, since Bretton Woods, and their implications for global and domestic development. In this respect use is made, for illustrative purposes, of the development experience of Nigeria and India: the former symbolizing a relatively open and the latter a relatively closed economy. The analysis provides for lessons of development policies and for the prospects for the 1990s and beyond. The book is aimed at supplementing existing texts on development. We hope that both graduate and postgraduate social scientists as well as those concerned with policy-making will be able to draw and build upon the major principles which emerge. To enable those who may not be development specialists grasp the key issues, technical language is kept to a minimum.

We extend our heartfelt thanks to Edward Elgar, our publisher, for his guidance and encouragement in initiating and completing the study, and to Julie Leppard, editor, for helpful advice throughout. We would also like to express our appreciation to an unknown referee for extremely helpful comments and suggestions for improving the manuscript.

The Institute of Development Studies, University of Sussex, has been an invaluable source of information and we are thankful to the library staff, and in particular to Bill Posnett, Sheila Watson and Barbara Degenhardt. Family and friends provided much needed encouragement at various stages of preparation. Bharati Roy, wife of one of the authors, was a source of constant motivation, while their son, Shoumyaroop, remained patient during the critical phases. Others including T.V. Sathyamurthy, Lalage Bown, Alfredo Barriga, David Okwuduli and Vincent Tickner also helped in their own way.

Thanks also go to Caroline Pybus for putting the manuscript together and to Joyce Stacey for proof-reading.

H.W. Singer and Sumit Roy

Introduction

Development[1], including growth and eradication of poverty and inequality, over the last 40 years, since Bretton Woods, has been uneven, and while some problems have been resolved, others have emerged requiring new solutions. The development process has been shaped by interaction between global and domestic policies, although their relative importance has varied among developing countries.[2]

The focus of this book is on analysing the major shifts and changes in development thinking and development strategy since Bretton Woods in the context of three linked periods: the 'golden age' of the 1950s and 1960s, the decade of 'illusionary debt-led growth' of the 1970s, and the 'lost decade' of the 1980s. This looks first at the global and second at the domestic level, the latter based on case studies of two major countries, Nigeria and India. The insights gained from the analysis are used to discuss the prospects for a 'decade of rehabilitation' in the 1990s.

The book is divided into three parts. Part 1 emphasizes the global context both actual and intellectual in which developing countries had to operate during the postwar period. Historical experience is discussed in the chronological frame of the three linked periods. Part 2 illustrates more fully the ways in which the key development thinking and in particular development strategy, discussed in Part 1, were used to stimulate growth and reduce poverty in the Nigerian and the Indian economy.[3] This is also placed in the frame of the three linked time periods and analyses the response of the countries to changes in external conditions.

Nigeria[4] and India[5] are here not used as typical or representative developing countries but because their experience of development provides scope for analysis of 'successes' and 'failures' of policies. Both are large countries, with low per capita income, a sizeable agricultural sector, and both have tried to industrialize. They have been integrated with the global economy, and embody features of open and closed economies. However, while Nigeria has been exposed relatively more to external forces, with outward-based policies playing a major role, India has been more protected pursuing primarily an inward-looking thrust. Both are 'mixed' economies, using state- and market-directed policies,[6] and the outcomes show similarities and contrasts. Their experience can provide useful lessons for development. These, however, need to be adapted to the specific situation of particular developing countries.[7]

Taken together, Part 1 and Part 2 throw light on the role of external factors and 'good governance'. Part 3 looks into the future. The experiences of the postwar period discussed in Part 1 and Part 2 show that throughout there were mixtures of opportunities and dangers. Part 3 explains that this is also likely to be true of the decade of the 1990s. There is now, however, a new agenda. Yet there are also items left over from the Bretton Woods agenda, and increasingly it is realized that the lessons of history are still relevant. The ideas and vision of a new international order of that time can still play an important role in shaping a better future. But even the more modest goal of making up for the setbacks in Latin America and Africa during the lost decade of the 1980s will present a formidable challenge. The case studies suggest that sustainable development will demand action on both the external front as well as improved domestic governance. In this respect, a more effective and democratic system of global management is essential.

Part 1, originally published as an IDS (Institute of Development Studies) Discussion Paper, and Part 3 were written by H.W. Singer. Part 2 was written by Sumit Roy.

NOTES

1. The literature on economic development can be divided into four major and sometimes competing approaches: (1) the linear stages of growth model; (2) theories and patterns of structural change; (3) the international dependency and Marxist analysis; (4) the neoclassical, free market 'counter-revolution'. The first emphasizes the quantity and mixture of saving, investment and foreign aid to bring about development, seen in terms of economic growth. The second portrays the internal process of structural change that a 'typical' developing country must undergo if it is to succeed in generating and sustaining a process of rapid economic growth. The third views underdevelopment in terms of international and domestic power relationships, institutional and structural economic rigidities. The fourth emphasizes the benefits of free markets and calls for reductions in government intervention in promoting development. See for example Todaro, 1989, pp. 63–4. Also see Hunt, 1989.
2. It is difficult to assess the relative contribution of external and internal factors in the response of a national economy to an economic disturbance. One extreme view is that developing countries are by and large blameless and perform poorly because of an adverse external environment. The other extreme is that all economic problems in developing countries are due to their own poor or inadequate policies. Generally speaking, reality is a complex mixture of the two. See Cooper, 1992, pp. 17–18. For a critique of some of the key studies on development at the global level and the need to incorporate the domestic level see Smith, 1982.
3. Basically, growth and poverty reduction are based on transformation from an agricultural to an industrial economy, and this is mirrored in the contribution of the key sectors to output, income and employment. The trade structure is also likely to show a shift in emphasis from exporting agricultural to industrial goods.

4. Nigeria has been described by Cooper as a relatively open country (Cooper, 1992, p. 97). With about 25 per cent of Africa's population, she is one of the most important ex-colonial African countries. She gained independence in 1960. Before the oil boom in the early 1970s, exports of agricultural commodities constituted the major source of foreign exchange earnings. Subsequently oil, with more favourable terms of trade, took their place (Watts, 1987, p. 2).

5. India has been described by Cooper as a relatively protectionist country (Cooper, 1992, p. 97). She gained independence in 1947. Her development experience over the last 40 years, with limited dependence on trade, is a mixture of 'successes' and 'failures'. India has been a challenge to development economics in particular and planners in all mixed economies. See Patel, 1985, p. 15.

6. Varying combinations of state and market forces guide the pursuit of development policies. The state embodies the instruments of power in society and hence access of different groups to the state has critical implications for shaping development policies. On the Indian state see Bardhan, 1984; on the Nigerian state see Beckman, 1982. On state intervention in both countries see Roy, 1990, pp. 22–3; pp. 43–6.

7. Thus, the lessons need to be related to the extent to which a country is open, its size, the contribution of the major sectors to gross domestic product, and the role of the state and the market in shaping development.

PART 1

Overall Postwar Development Experience, 1945–89*

*This Part was originally published in 1989 as *IDS Discussion Paper* no. 260.

Introduction

This first part traces the development process from the creation of the Bretton Woods institutions to present-day adjustment measures: from the optimism of the postwar era to the present scenario of adjustment, retrenchment and stabilization. What were the mistakes and the success stories, and the lessons that can be drawn from them these last 40 years? This part assesses how and why the Bretton Woods institutions fell short of their initial aims; it takes a hard look at the 'golden years' of the 1950s and 1960s; it analyses the 'debt-led' growth of the 1970s and the resulting 'lost decade' of the 1980s in Africa and Latin America. It goes on to examine the successes and failures that emerge from the history of the development process, and argues in favour of learning these lessons by resuming a policy of 'redistribution with growth' and re-establishing strong international institutions to ensure future growth in developing countries.

1. The Story of Development: Differing Scenarios

The story of development, the lessons of development experience, the evolution of our thinking about development – all these things (which are not exactly the same) can be written from many different angles. One could start the story with the high hopes for a Brave New World at the end of the Second World War at Bretton Woods; comparing these hopes with the 'lost decade' of the 1980s, with its debt crisis, African crisis and development going into reverse – at least in Africa and Latin America. The story could then be written as one of clear deterioration, of the Brave New World of 40 years ago ending in a developmental wasteland today. But that story would certainly not be wholly true. It would not do justice to the many success stories in development, nor to the 'golden years' spanning over two decades after Bretton Woods, nor to the fact that measured by such simple but compelling indicators as expectation of life, infant mortality, technological capacity, or progress with industrialization, the Third World as a whole is markedly better off than 40 years ago.

Another possible scenario when surveying the last 40 years could be as a story of ups and downs, of problems emerging and being solved, or left unresolved, only to be replaced by other problems requiring different solutions. This would be somewhat nearer the truth than the first account. The development story is clearly a mixture of good and bad, of progress and regress, of success and failure. Indeed, it is this very mixture which leads to much confusion. Some people, institutions or schools of thought tend to pick out the failures and draw from them lessons of what should be done to redeem them or avoid them in the future. Others will be more inclined to point out successes, and base their conclusions on what should be done to extend and support them. Obviously both approaches are justified: we should learn both from success and failure. But in practice, this polarized approach often leads to unhelpful debates with arguments based on selective anecdotal evidence. This can result in inconclusive controversies, for example whether aid is beneficial or harmful to developing countries; whether the cause of the troubles of developing countries is internal or external; whether developing countries should practise inward or outward orientation; whether developing countries should use modern capital-intensive technology or traditional labour-intensive technology, etc.

Generally, it is unhelpful to pose such questions and try to answer them in this polarized or categorical form of 'either/or'. The truth broadly is that the right kind of aid is good and the wrong kind bad; that inward orientation is right for certain countries, certain sectors and in certain conditions and outward orientation for other countries, sectors and conditions, while usually a selective and phased mixture of inward-oriented and outward-oriented measures is best; a selective mixture or 'blending' of modern and traditional technology is best; in the present debt crisis internal factors play a role and interact with external factors, etc. The problem is that in such polarized controversies the advocacy of either of the two alternatives often assumes the nature of a religious conviction, argued with fundamentalist passion. When one of these factions acquires ascendancy in and control over important institutions and governments it can do much harm. One illustration of this is the fervent belief in planning, the possibilities of the 'big push' and 'balanced growth' and import-substituting industrialization some 40 years ago; and the perhaps even more fanatical belief in outward orientation, market power and 'getting prices right' which has succeeded today in capturing the stage in powerful international institutions and governments. One can observe that the success stories tend to be based on a cool disregard of such fundamentalism – not so much a 'search for a middle ground' as a selective use of the elements of truth contained in either of the contending doctrines.

This last point could well suggest a third scenario: one in which our approach to development problems and the lessons which we learn is simply the result of changing fashions and ideologies. If it was the Keynesian consensus 40 years ago, it is now the neo-liberal tide or 'Washington consensus' of today, and goodness knows what tomorrow. This scenario, familiar to historians, is the counterpart of the proposition that history is not a logical evolution in which events in epoch B are linked with events in the preceding epoch A and will in turn be linked with future events in epoch C; but rather that history is 'just one damn thing after another'. Yet this again does not quite seem the whole truth. There was a sense in which the belief in planning and self-reliance in the 1940s and 1950s was based on the experience of the war and the preceding Great Depression; in which the later move towards outward orientation was based on the expansion of the world economy and world trade in the 1950s and 1960s; in which the temporarily successful OPEC action of 1973 and 1979 was linked with the experience of deteriorating and unstable terms of trade; in which the debt crisis of today is linked to the OPEC action and the response of the industrial countries to this action; in which the present African crisis is linked to the historical experience of new independence and the difficulties of giving political independence a proper economic meaning and foundation. So perhaps the story of development is more than just 'one damn thing after another'; it is a story of unfolding, of one thing leading to another in a process which can be given some meaning. But the trouble seems to be one of time lags. Just as generals tend to fight the last-but-one war, so the development actors as well as the development thinkers seem to base their action and thought on experiences of the last-but-one decade or a last-but-one phase, only to be overwhelmed by the inappropriateness of such action and thought in the face of new events and new problems. Is it perhaps a case of a problem for every solution, rather than a solution for every problem?

This seems to come close to the truth. It can be presented pessimistically as always reacting too late and to an obsolete situation; or more optimistically as a learning process. We react – although inevitably with a time lag – to the lessons of the past. Perhaps we can also learn to speed up this learning process, to react more quickly and more relevantly to new events. Even more optimistically, we can describe the last 40 years as a journey of discovery. For example, from an earlier emphasis on physical capital accumulation we have all – planners, Keynesians, neo-liberals, structuralists or whatever we call ourselves – learnt to attribute greater importance to human capital; similarly we are all agreed – at least theoretically – to attribute more importance to reduction of poverty than to mere growth of GNP. The trouble is that while we may share in such discoveries, we still differ widely about what conclusions to draw for development policy. We all want to reduce poverty and enable people to live up to their full potential, but that does not guarantee any agreement about the policies best designed to achieve these common objectives. Instead they take their place alongside mother love and apple pie as emotional invocations. The ritual invocation of such common objectives may become a rhetorical mask. The 'human face' may become merely a face-lift for any policies which we advocate; the same may be true of the description of all types of adjustment policies as 'growth-oriented'.

The scenario which is, perhaps, the most fruitful approach to an understanding of the development story and to drawing proper lessons from it, is the one indicated by the motto from Dr Johnson which precedes the next section: 'Seldom any splendid story is wholly true'. This seems to fit the last 40 years. Compared with the prewar and wartime situation, it *is* a 'splendid story'. The world today would be a worse place without it. Yet the splendid story that emerged was not 'wholly true'; it was incomplete, flawed and its defects carried the germ of its own destruction. Our problem then is to live up to the scenario of development as a learning process and create a new 'splendid story'. That, at any rate, is the angle from which we will now look at the story of development.

2. The High Hopes of Bretton Woods and the Worm in the Apple

'Seldom any splendid story is wholly true.' (Dr Johnson)

At the end of the Second World War there was clearly a unique opportunity to reshape the world international system. The old order had been swept away. There was a burning desire to learn the lessons of recent experience and avoid the errors of judgement and policies which were felt to be among the causes of the disastrous war. So, clearly the new system created at Bretton Woods and in the UN reflected the current perceptions of the immediate prewar and wartime experience. What were these perceptions?

First, there was the perceived need to avoid the disastrous beggar-my-neighbour policies of the 1930s when countries, dominated by traditional and classical doctrines of reliance on 'equilibrating' market mechanisms, got themselves deeper and deeper into competitive devaluations, heavy deflation, rising unemployment, and protectionism, with their terrible social and political consequences. (Perhaps this lesson now needs to be relearned.) Between 1929 and 1933 world trade declined in value by 65 per cent and in volume by 25 per cent. The belief in classical policies had been swept away by a new Keynesian consensus on active macroeconomic management by governments, with full employment set as the primary objective. In the international field, the conclusion drawn was that nationalist policies must be replaced by international rules of conduct and control by international institutions.

The 1930s had also been accompanied by a disastrous fall in primary commodity prices, and the lesson drawn by Keynes and others at the time was the need to stabilize primary commodity prices. For that purpose, it was decided at Bretton Woods that in addition to the IMF and World Bank, a third international organization was needed – the ITO, or International Trade Organization – with the dual purpose of stabilizing primary commodity prices and promoting world trade.

The wartime experience of the industrial countries had demonstrated the potential for macroeconomic planning and effective government action to maximize output, mobilize latent resources, achieve full employment, and at the same time control inflation and achieve more equal income distribution.

This experience was particularly striking in the case of the UK which, in the person of Keynes, played a dominant intellectual role in the creation of the Bretton Woods system. There was a strong feeling that the same principles of planning, macroeconomic management of the economy by governments and mobilization of latent resources based on Keynesian principles, were also applicable to the problems of developing countries. These had become a more important item of world interest as a result of the emergence into independence of the countries of the Indian sub-continent and a shift in colonial policies in Africa towards preparation for independence. For many in the West, it seemed natural to extend the principles of the welfare state from the national to the international sphere, and the idea of international income transfers, including large-scale multilateral transfers centred in the UN, began to take shape.

Bretton Woods was indeed a 'splendid story'. It was an immense improvement over the situation of the 1930s; it gave us 25 'golden years' – from 1948 until the early 1970s when the Bretton Woods system broke down – as will be presently shown.

The success of the new system was not entirely due to its intrinsic value. The Marshall Plan (1948–52) had a great deal to do with creating a period over two decades when the industrial countries, through steady growth at a rate of 5 per cent or more, with full employment, little inflation and balance of payments disequilibria solved first by the Marshall Plan, then by US investment and later by a strong recovery of exports and the emerging balance of payments surpluses of Europe and Japan, provided a firm foundation (or 'engine') for the growth of production and exports in developing countries, enabling them to maintain on aggregate growth rates similar to or even higher than those of the industrial countries (although not on a per capita basis). World trade expanded even faster than GNP, and protectionist incentives were minimized.

If the Marshall Plan had demonstrated the potential effectiveness of large-scale international income transfers, the response of Europe in presenting joint programmes and moving towards trade liberalization in the form of a common market also seemed to demonstrate the possibility of constructive recipient policies and collaboration between donors and recipients. So in the first days of high hopes for the Brave New World, development activists in the UN and elsewhere began to think in terms of multi-annual, large-scale aid of the Marshall type for developing countries, linked to the GNP of the industrial countries and thus increasing at the same steady rate of 5 per cent per annum or more in line with industrial countries' GNP. A target of 1 per cent of GNP then seemed to be quite modest – the USA, under the Marshall Plan, had transferred something more like 3 per cent of its GNP for four years running. While it was recognized and admitted from the beginning that development problems would be more difficult and longer term than the reconstruction of Europe and Japan, this was assumed to be offset by the strengthening of donor capacity, as the beneficiaries of the Marshall Plan would 'graduate' to large-scale donors. Moreover, the capital transfers could be partly in the form of private investment: the prevailing perception was that there should be plenty of scope for productive investment in developing countries since the marginal productivity of capital must be higher in these capital-scarce countries. However, private investment was assumed to be the junior partner to Marshall Plan-type aid (later, in the first UN Development Decade, quantified as 0.3:0.7).

Where, then, was the worm in the apple? Why did the splendid story not come wholly true? The most obvious defect was that the Bretton Woods system remained incomplete. To begin with, the International Trade Organization (ITO) which Keynes had considered to be an indispensable third pillar of the Bretton Woods system, never came into being. Although it was duly negotiated and agreed at Havana, the 'Havana Charter' was not ratified by the US Congress. This was largely a matter of time lags – by the time the ITO was ready for ratification, the climate of opinion in the USA had changed: the Roosevelt/Truman era in which 'freedom from want' had been proclaimed as a global objective, was beginning to shade into the very different McCarthy era in which the UN and all its works became 'an evil empire'. Another reason why the ITO was not ratified was the fact that commodity prices had temporarily risen, as a result first of postwar shortages and then of the Korean War, so that intervention by the ITO seemed unnecessary.

Some of the intended functions of the ITO were subsequently shifted to GATT (the General Agreement on Tariffs and Trade); but GATT was a weak version, and in some ways a perversion, of the intended ITO – a negotiating mechanism rather than an instrument of multilateral action – and did not include the vital function of commodity price stabilization. In fact GATT emasculated the trade policy chapter in the Havana Charter, deleting not only the chapters on commodity agreements, but also those on employment, development and restrictive business practices. GATT became – and to some extent remained – very much a first world institution, and initially failed to make any allowances for the special problems of developing countries. Nor did the subsequent creation of UNCTAD in 1964 fill the gap left by the failure of the ITO; by that time the shift in economic power and relevance away from the UN was complete and the industrial countries were determined to keep UNCTAD at the level of a talking shop. However some useful initiatives subsequently came from UNCTAD, particularly the acceptance of the GSP – the Generalized System of Preferences. In fact this initiative was probably more useful to developing countries than all the 'trade liberalizations' under GATT which were largely offset by the growth of non-tariff restrictions outside the GATT system, including the MFA – Multi-Fibre Agreement – and the so-called 'voluntary' export restraints.

The even more far-reaching plans for commodity stabilization proposed by Keynes never had a real political chance to materialize. Keynes had proposed a world currency to be based not on gold, not on the dollar, not on sterling, not on SDRs, but on 30 primary commodities (including oil and gold); this would automatically have stabilized at least the average price of these 30 commodities. But however ripe the situation at the end of the war was for a Brave New World, this Ultra-New World proposed by Keynes proved to be too radical; at Bretton Woods it sank without trace. Perhaps Keynes would have fought harder for it if he had known that the ITO would not come into existence, but by the time this had become clear, Keynes was dead, and in any case, the enthusiasm for a Brave New World had largely evaporated.

The Bretton Woods system was also incomplete in that the UN, which was supposed to be another pillar of the Bretton Woods system, was never brought into action in the way initially expected. This was largely due to the adverse change in the political climate already referred to. The initial hope was that a 'special fund' should be set up in the UN to administer large-scale soft aid, more or less on Marshall Plan terms, to developing countries. This proposal, originating in the UN Sub-Commission for Economic Development in 1948, was taken up in more detail in the 1951 Report of the UN Expert Group (which included two subsequent Nobel Laureates, Arthur Lewis and Ted Schultz) on 'Measures for Economic Development'. Although the process of detailed preparations and negotiations was duly set in motion in the UN system and the statute for a 'UN Fund for Economic Development' was laboriously evolved, under the chairmanship of the subsequent UN Secretary General U Thant, the unfortunate initials of this proposed fund, i.e. UNFED, described only too well the fate awaiting this stillbirth. (When it was realized how the initials would be received, the word 'Special' was hastily put in front – but unfortunately the science fiction nature of the new acronym of SUNFED still provided an all too accurate description of the chances of its success.) The long opposition of the World Bank not only to involving the UN in financial aid but even to the principle of soft aid, also served to prevent this idea materializing. When, with the dawn of the more liberal Kennedy era, the chances for soft, multilateral aid became better and the World Bank dropped its opposition to it, it was clear that the Western donor countries would not be willing to channel it through the UN where the developing countries had a major say, but through the World Bank which the donors controlled. In any case, the new IDA (International Development Association) never reached dimensions remotely comparable with the Marshall Plan. At the same time, the UN received two valuable consolation prizes in the form of being allocated food aid (the World Food Programme) and technical assistance (the UNDP). In fact, the UNDP initially, before its merger with ETAP (the UN Expanded Technical Assistance Programme arising from point IV), still carried in its name of 'Special Fund', a recognition of the aborted SUNFED. But that was meagre consolation compared with the initial hopes. So the Bretton Woods system which was meant to walk on four legs (UN, ITO, IMF and the World Bank) was hobbling along on the last two only.

Not only was the Bretton Woods structure incomplete, it was also distorted. In Keynes's original vision, and in line with his high priority for avoiding deflation and recession, he had suggested an IMF which would put adjustment pressure on balance of payments surplus countries rather than deficit countries. This was to be achieved by making it mandatory for surpluses to be held in a World Central Bank, and for these deposits of surpluses to carry a negative rate of interest (i.e. to be taxed). Although this vision is still partly reflected in the constitution of the IMF, enjoining it to put equal pressure on deficit and surplus countries, the IMF has proved utterly incapable of exerting pressure on surplus countries – neither Japan and Germany today nor OPEC in the 1970s. The pressure is now entirely concentrated on deficit countries, which are asked to 'put their house in order'; even among these the pressure is selective, and the IMF makes no significant impact on the biggest balance of payments deficit country of today – the USA. Any admonition of industrial countries, and specifically the surplus countries, to 'put their house in order' remains entirely at the rhetorical level; there is no question of conditionality or financial sanctions.

There is of course an historical explanation – to some extent an alibi – for this distortion of original intentions. The Keynesian desire to put pressure on surplus countries was based on the undesirability of deflationary pressures in times of unemployment and recession: in such conditions, the surplus country is the enemy of the world economy and should be penalized, while the deficit country is the friend of the world economy and should be supported. During the golden years of full employment this prescription, of course, was no longer appropriate; pressure on deficit countries was then justified. The trouble is that with the shift in the world situation to slow growth, unemployment and recessions after 1973, the IMF has not returned – or has not been allowed to return – to the policies originally recommended with the Great Depression of the 1930s in mind, and which now, once again, were appropriate in the light of the economic situation since 1973. In this respect the time-lag scenario previously presented would seem applicable: Keynes's proposals were made to cope with the recessionary situation of the 1930s; these proposals were then reversed to deal with the different situation of the

1950s and 1960s, but this reversal was then maintained, and indeed intensi-fied, in a new economic climate when it was no longer appropriate.

There seems little prospect, however, that this process of 'learning, but too late' will be continued in the future. In the absence of a world central bank, world currency and global source of liquidity which can be realized or withheld – all these part of the Keynesian proposals – it is difficult to see how even in the future the Bretton Woods institutions could put effective pressure on surplus countries. It would certainly require a dramatic reform of the system in the direction suggested by Keynes. Interestingly enough, there are some faint signs of recognition of what has been lost: for example, in the case of the ITO there is the Compensatory Financing Facility and the recent addition of commodity prices to the list of IMF indicators – the beginning of a recognition that debt repayment capacity and structural ad-justment capabilities are tied to terms of trade. There is again talk of devel-oping GATT into a World Trade Organization (WTO) as well as the possibility of making a reality of the embryonic Common Fund created by UNCTAD.

3. The 1950s and 1960s: Were They Really Solid Gold?

The 1950s and 1960s were a period of global expansion of production and trade, one of the longest and most pronounced booms in world history, with full employment and little inflation in the industrial countries. This was a favourable environment for developing countries, including those gaining independence during that period. This was fully reflected in the statistical and aggregate picture of development, with increases in output, trade, technological capacity, acquisition of planning experience and so on. In many developing countries this period saw the rise of a middle class and the development of entrepreneurship. All the same, the approach to development, based as it was on prewar and wartime experiences and on the incomplete Bretton Woods system, and to a large extent a reflection of the progress of the industrial countries, showed certain weaknesses which were to become apparent in the course of time, and from which some lessons could be drawn. However, sometimes the actual lessons learnt were based on 'yesterday', i.e. they came too late to be appropriate to newly changed circumstances.

Some of the characteristic approaches to development during the golden years have already been mentioned. To begin with there was a heavy and almost exclusive emphasis on physical capital accumulation. The Keynesian consensus ruled supreme, and the neo-Keynesian development model, embodied in the Harrod–Domar formula, emphasized capital accumulation as the source of growth, with the capital/output ratio in the denominator of the formula being taken more or less as constant. This emphasis on physical capital accumulation also drew support from Russian planning and its apparent successes. This virtually exclusive emphasis was perhaps most clearly expressed by Maurice Dobb lecturing to the Delhi School of Economics in 1951:

> The largest single factor governing productivity in a country is its richness or poorness in capital instruments of production. And I think that we shall not go far wrong if we treat capital accumulation, in the sense of a growth in the stock of capital instruments – a growth that is simultaneously qualitative and quantitative – as the crux of the process of economic development.

This emphasis on capital accumulation was almost universally shared: it was also clearly embodied in the approach underlying the previously mentioned proposals of the UN experts in 1951. Subsequently, and in the light of experience, it was found that the 'capital/output ratio' can be a very troublesome factor. It may have an obstinate tendency to remain unfavourable, i.e. high, or even to rise; it is largely governed by 'human' factors such as education, skill, training, health, nutrition and so on not explicit in the Harrod–Domar model; and much of the physical capital accumulation, at least in the earlier stages, is of the infrastructure type, with high capital/output ratios and long maturity periods needed for a full return. Moreover, contrary to the optimistic belief, based on external economies and the theory of balanced growth, that capital/output ratios would rapidly decline as investment expands, other factors may intervene in the opposite direction: for example, increased investment may outrun the technical and administrative capacity of a country to design, implement and operate efficient development projects. The smaller size and lack of economies of scale could also be relevant for developing countries. So the initial equation of development with physical capital accumulation led to increasing problems and was increasingly questioned as the golden years went on.

A more mature synthesis later emerged in which physical and human capital formation were seen as both necessary and neither sufficient, and emphasis was laid on their interaction. Familiarity with physical capital and its operation will help to develop human skills, just as educated and skilled labour will improve the operation of physical capital and suggest lines of technical progress.

Emphasis on physical capital accumulation was linked with optimism regarding the domestic capacity of developing countries and their governments to mobilize domestic savings and investment, and an equally optimistic belief that this might be supplemented by large foreign aid injections on the precedent of the Marshall Plan. Domestic capital accumulation was to be promoted by utilization of surplus labour, especially in agriculture, and utilization of the potential of 'disguised unemployment'. Such confidence that domestic savings and investment could be rapidly increased was not entirely misplaced. In fact, domestic savings and investment ratios in most developing countries increased quite rapidly and soon reached and exceeded the rather modest initial targets set for them (which in turn were based on optimistic assumptions for capital/output ratios). However, it turned out that quite often the source of the increased domestic savings and investment was not so much the mobilization of latent surplus labour (which would have been a factor making for an egalitarian pattern of development), but rather an emerging inequality of income distribution and a squeezing of the agricultural sector (making for an inegalitarian pattern of development and long-term problems with demand for manufactured goods).

As for the hoped-for Marshall-type flow of external resources which was supposed to supplement domestic savings and prevent balance of payments difficulties, this failed to materialize. The failure of an attempt at a Marshall Plan under UN auspices, in the name of SUNFED, has already been described. In any case, it is doubtful whether an injection of the Marshall Plan type, whether bilateral or multilateral, would have had the same effect in developing countries as in Europe. The lesson of the Marshall Plan was that such injections are most effective where the recipients come forward with their own proposals and agree in advance on the division and use of the external funds; where the recipients are willing to use the funds as the basis for increased cooperation among themselves; where there is already the human basis in terms of skill, experience and education; and where there is a high degree of technological capacity among the recipients. None of these conditions would have been present in a Marshall Plan for the developing countries during the golden period. Perhaps today the preconditions would be better, but the sad fact is that a Marshall Plan today would not be devoted so much to development as to solving the debt crisis and to damage limitation from the setbacks of the 1980s.

The type of external resource which did, in fact, flow in excess of expectations was private capital. The target for the First Development Decade of the 1960s was for aid to constitute 70 per cent of the total inflow, more than double the private inflow. However, the situation was more or less reversed. This substitution of private capital for official aid at concessional terms had obvious implications for future balances of payments: the seeds of the future debt problem were sown. Moreover, in so far as much of this private inflow represented direct investment by multinational corporations, often in the form of subsidiaries, some of the growth of the golden years inevitably acquired an exogenous, and often enclave, character rather than representing truly national capacity. Towards the end of the period, debates developed around whether the transfer of technology connected with such direct foreign investment was a valuable bonus of such investment and had national demonstration effects; or whether, on the contrary, it introduced inappropriate technology, stifled local enterprise and technology and encouraged a brain drain from developing countries. It also meant that some of the rents accruing to protected import-substituting industries were expatriated as profits of foreign subsidiaries, with strain on the balance of payments, thus nullifying the saving of foreign exchange through import substitution. But the same also applied to more export-oriented types of industrialization. In so far as the exports came from foreign subsidiaries, the degree of retention of the foreign exchange earned from exports was clearly reduced. The share of foreign subsidiaries in exports of NICs (newly industrialized countries) towards the end of the golden era was estimated at 15–30 per cent for South Korea, 40–50 per cent for Brazil, 25–30 per cent for Mexico and 70–85 per cent for Singapore.

Another reason (apart from excessive expectations of aid inflows) why insufficient attention was often paid to possible balance of payments constraints was that at the beginning of the golden years commodity prices were buoyant, with a peak in 1951 at the time of the Korean War. Also, many developing countries had accumulated important foreign exchange reserves during the war which could be gradually drawn upon. This happy situation did not last however: terms of trade and relative prices of primary commodities deteriorated quite sharply during the golden years, resuming their declining prewar trend. This took quite a lot of steam out of the great savings and investment effort; development turned out to be an uphill struggle, and the possibility of 'immiserizing growth' began to raise its ugly head. The single-gap neo-Keynesian formula which made growth dependent only on the rate of investment began to be replaced by 'dual gap' theories of development where the balance of payments appeared as a separate and often dominant constraining factor. Thus, for balance of payments reasons, success in raising domestic savings rates could turn sour in that the potential savings capacity could not be fully utilized for lack of foreign exchange. Here, the failure of aid to reach the modest targets set, let alone the dimensions of a 'Marshall Plan', came increasingly to be felt as a constraining factor.

Another consequence of the poor experience with primary commodity prices during the period immediately before the war was a certain export pessimism which contrasted sharply with domestic optimism. This export pessimism led to emphasis on industrialization as the most obvious diversification out of primary commodities – not just any kind of industrialization but that with an emphasis on import substitution. As far as reliance on exports of primary commodities was concerned, this pessimism was largely justified by events: in spite of unprecedented expansion in the industrial countries, the terms of trade for primary commodities fell by over 25 per cent between 1951 and 1965 and volume also expanded much less than might have been expected. Where the pessimism proved to be unjustified, however, was in being extended to all exports. This was based partly on the prewar experience of recession in the industrial countries and shrinking world trade, and partly on a belief that exports of manufactures were largely beyond the reach of developing countries. The first assumption turned out to be quite false: in contrast to the prewar shrinkage, world trade bounced ahead at rates considerably exceeding even the high growth rates of industrial countries. But the second assumption was largely justified at the time:

in the early 1950s it was very difficult to visualize the rapid expansion of exports of manufactures from the NICs, India, Brazil and other developing countries beginning in the 1960s. Much of the infrastructure needed for export industries was simply not there; such industries would have lacked the foundation of a domestic market which still had to be created by planning for balanced growth. With the benefit of hindsight and in the light of experience, we can now say that developing countries did not pay sufficient attention during the golden years to the possibilities of export substitution rather than import substitution, i.e. moving from exports of primary commodities into exports of manufactured goods. As a corollary, not enough attention was paid by many developing countries to the need to keep the import-substituting industries efficient so that they could rapidly develop into export industries. In fact, the methods adopted to establish import-substituting industries were often directly hostile to the development of efficiency as a basis for subsequent exports.

There is a long list of factors now recognized as creating such a danger of inefficient import substitution. This list would include rent seeking rather than efficiency as a basis of profits in protected import-substituting industries; encouragement of foreign penetration of the economy, leading to the elimination of local producers and preventing indigenous learning processes; a tendency to adopt imported capital-intensive technologies; concentration on items of luxury consumption of the type previously imported; and absence of sufficient vertical deepening of the import-substituting industries, in particular a failure to develop local capital goods industries.

Such a catalogue of sins is fashionable today as a basis for arguing that industrialization should have been more 'export led' or 'outward oriented' from the beginning. However, one should be careful before drawing this particular lesson from the experience of the 1950s and 1960s. To begin with, when exports of manufactures did start in a promising way in the 1960s, they were often based on industries originally developed as import substitutes, or at any rate for the domestic market; many of the export industries were only possible on the basis of previous infrastructure investment in transport, education, and so on. The technological capacity for successful export competition in manufactures had to be built up by industrial experience gained from industrialization for the domestic market.

Moreover, even today it can be shown that 'outward orientation' works better as a recipe for middle-income countries than for low-income countries – and in the 1950s practically all developing countries were still in the category of what are now considered to be low-income countries. There is a clear danger that the lesson of 'outward orientation' will be learned in a less favourable international climate than during the golden years and then become counter-productive. There is also a fallacy of composition in jumping from the success stories of some countries in exporting manufactures to the conclusion that all or most developing countries could have followed the same strategies with the same results.

The emphasis on industrialization was right (within limits to be discussed) and the emphasis on substitution, i.e. substituting manufactured goods for primary commodities, was also right. But the possibilities of export substitution were underrated. Although this did not prevent a vigorous participation of developing countries as a whole in world trade in manufactures at a later stage, it did mean that when the time came, this participation was concentrated on a relatively small number of developing countries.

Probably the most important weakness of the import-substituting industrialization strategy was that it did not really substitute for imports. Due to the lack of vertical integration, it shifted imports from finished products to inputs of intermediate and capital goods, saving very little foreign exchange in the process. However, the same objection can also be raised about the later export-led success stories, like South Korea and the other East Asian 'tigers': the net value added by exports was often only a small fraction of the statistical export value, with a high proportion of the exports being offset by imports of necessary inputs to produce these exports. The chief difference, however, was that whereas import substitution tended to run out of steam when the simpler and final-stage imports had been substituted, in the case of export-led growth, the import content of the exports was steadily reduced in the case of the tigers and also of some of the Latin American countries (as happened before in Japan), so that the net value added represented by a given value of exports was steadily increased. However, it must remain an open question to what extent this difference is due to the superiority of outward orientation over inward orientation, or to what extent it is due to the fact that both import substitution and export promotion were handled with greater efficiency in the case of the successful countries, helped by third factors such as standards of education, promotion of indigenous technology, administrative efficiency of the government, entrepreneurial culture, labour discipline and so on. There must be a presumption that such third factors were important, because in most of the outward-oriented success stories one will also find that the import-substitution industries developed to a high level of efficiency (many of them becoming export industries) and that these outward-oriented countries relied heavily on import substitution in the earlier stages and continue to do so with proper selectivity. Proper selectivity, overall efficiency, proper timing and phasing, the ability to 'pick winners' seemed to be more important elements of successful development than any so-called inward or outward orientation.

The neo-classical 'new orthodoxy' has revived the myth of the passive state. The active developmental state supposedly just retards growth by creating widespread inefficiencies, stifling enterprise and preventing market signals from functioning. Governments should move towards limiting their role to ensuring 'sound money' and 'getting the prices right'. Yet the success stories belie such an interpretation. The East Asian NICs, and especially South Korea, have had extensive state intervention throughout their development in industrial planning, infrastructure, training, finance and labour relations, with subsidization of some industries and protection of others. As Amartya Sen has commented: 'If this is the free market, then Walras's auctioneer can surely be seen as going around with a government white paper in one hand and a whip in the other.' This is not to deny the importance of private sector dynamism, but the strategic role of the state was crucial. It is not the size of the state that is the real issue, but rather its roles and effectiveness. In practice this is acknowledged by many neo-classical economists.

In any case, much of the import-substituting and inward-looking nature of the early industrialization was the almost inevitable result of the political situation. This was clearly true in countries like India. The independence struggle had been intimately mixed up with protection against the imports from industrial countries destroying local and traditional industries: Gandhi's spinning wheel and boycott of textile imports from Lancashire are symbolic. The linkage between national independence and inward-looking industrialization was also due to the political perception that national independence and sovereignty are meaningless without a measure of industrialization and self-sufficiency. This perception was to be repeated in the 1960s in the newly independent African countries with economically even more unsatisfactory results, because of the absence of many preconditions for successful industrialization compared with Asia or Latin America. If this process of import-substituting industrialization is looked at as a political necessity, much of the criticism of the process as being economically inferior loses in relevance.

The emphasis on physical capital accumulation as the 'crux' of development also led, in due course, to a tolerance for income inequalities and the persistence of poverty. This took the form either of a belief that growth was sooner or later bound to 'trickle down' and spread to the poor, or even more strongly, that increased income inequalities were a necessary price to pay for the time being until the luxury of welfare could be afforded from an enlarged cake of production. During this period of the 1950s and 1960s Kuznets's famous 'inverted U-curve' played a big role, and seemed to show that in the earlier stages of development, income inequalities increased until a turning point was reached – presumably at middle-income levels, perhaps after the 'take-off stage' identified by Rostow – when income distribution would become more equal again, and poverty would rapidly recede under the dual impact of a larger cake and a more equal income distribution. The same idea of a turning point away from inequality towards greater equality and welfare was also inherent in the Arthur Lewis model of development with surplus labour, which was very influential during this period. As the golden years went on, however, the existence of such a turning point at a reasonably early development stage became more and more doubtful. There seemed little sign either of trickle down or of a turning point in most of the developing countries. Hence new strategies of 'redistribution with growth' and more directly employment- and poverty-targeted approaches came to the fore, as will be described in the next section.

The Arthur Lewis model was also indicative of another weakness in the type of development prevalent during the golden years, namely a comparative neglect of agriculture. In this model and much related thinking, the main function of agriculture was to provide rural surplus labour as the cannon fodder of industrialization (reminiscent of what happened in the pioneer days of the Industrial Revolution in Great Britain), to provide a market for industrial goods and to provide the raw materials for processing by the prominent textile, leather and other industries. This passive or negative role ascribed to agriculture was never very convincing: how could agriculture provide a market for industrial goods unless rural incomes were raised? How could agriculture release surplus labour unless productivity was increased? How could growth trickle down to the poor when the great mass of the poor lived in rural areas? These and similar questions were not clearly faced, let alone answered.

There were several reasons for this blind spot in the early industrialization drive. One was the justified pessimism about relative prices of primary and agricultural products, which was perhaps too unthinkingly extended from the international to the domestic arena. There was also a strong belief (derived from classical credentials) that technical progress in agriculture would always be much slower and more difficult than in industry. This belief has proved unjustified, as shown by the tremendous increases in agricultural productivity in North America, Europe and the Far East, where technical progress in agriculture proved to be at least as fast as in industry, as well as the green revolution in some parts of the Third World.

Another reason was more political: an 'urban bias' injected into development policies by the disproportionate political influence of the urban minority compared with the rural majority. The opposite 'rural bias' in the agricultural policies followed in North America, Europe and Japan provided yet another reason for comparative neglect of agriculture in developing countries: it reduced international food prices, making imports easier and more tempting. It also made available during this period of surplus massive US food aid, enabling governments so inclined to justify low investment priorities for national food production. However, all the very large recipients of food aid during the 1950s and early 1960s, such as India, South Korea, Israel and Greece, eventually managed to use the resources provided by massive aid, including food aid, to provide the infrastructure investment for their own green revolutions. In this they followed in the footsteps of Western Europe and Japan, who also very quickly graduated out of the massive food aid provided by the Marshall Plan into becoming substantial surplus producers with strong 'rural bias' policies.

Overvalued exchange rates, often typical of countries engaged in import-substituting industrialization, work to the disadvantage not only of export industries but more particularly of agriculture, both by reducing exports and facilitating competing imports. So in the total picture of relative neglect of agriculture it was not surprising that the heavy net agricultural exports of developing countries began to fade as the period went on and net food exports were steadily converted into net food imports (although the agricultural policies of the richer countries had as much – or more – to do with this than the policies of developing countries).

Yet another phenomenon became apparent towards the second golden decades which served to take off some of the gilt, and was subsequently to become a source of great trouble and worry. This was an increasing divergence among developing countries. Growth turned out to be distinctly faster and easier among the middle-income countries than among the low-income countries. This remains true even when the circular nature of this relationship is taken into account, i.e. that faster growth pushes countries into the middle-income category while slower growth condemns countries to stay in the low-income category. Thus, during the last five years of the period (1965–70), the per capita income of middle-income countries, growing at 3.8 per cent per annum, increased almost twice as fast as the low-income countries, at 2.2 per cent. In fact, the middle-income developing countries grew slightly faster than the industrial market economies, even in per capita terms. It was the low-income countries which were beginning to fall behind. Thus the gap opening up during that period was not so much between North and South, but rather between the upper- and middle-income countries on the one hand, and the low-income countries on the other. The sub-category of what later came to be known as 'least developed countries' began to emerge, and so did a geographical concentration of this sub-category among the then very recently independent countries of sub-Saharan Africa. 'Marginalization' and the 'economic underclass' crept into the development agenda.

Another worrying feature of the golden years was the fact that in spite of rapid growth, increasing inflationary pressures and an international environment which should have been very favourable to primary commodity prices, they obstinately refused to improve relative to the price of manufactures imported by developing countries. Again, the least developed countries were the worst sufferers since they depended almost entirely on exports of primary products and, in the case of many African countries, on a single primary product. This seemed to reveal a structurally persistent weakness boding ill in the event of the kind of deterioration in the international climate which was to follow. Also, the suspicion arose, based on the emerging evidence of the 1960s, that even those developing countries which had engaged in successful export substitution of simple manufactures, typically textiles, shoes, processed primary products and so on, for primary exports did not seem to escape the threat of adverse terms of trade. An uneven distribution of gains from international trade was beginning to be seen to be not just a matter of different types of commodities but also of different types of countries, different degrees of technological power and different types of labour markets.

To sum up the experience of the golden years: the favourable growth experience, particularly for the middle-income countries, had certainly demonstrated the possibility of economic growth. This was more important than it might seem, since initially considerable doubt existed, both among politicians and economists, as to whether economic growth was not 'naturally' limited to *homo economicus* – economic man as existing in the industrial countries of the temperate zone. Newly independent countries in particular were viewed rather sceptically as to their growth possibilities. So this demonstration of the golden years of growth feasibility was no mean achievement; at any rate, the voices doubting the possibility of growth outside the sacred circle of the North were no longer heard towards the end of the period. Moreover, understanding of development problems had increased considerably during the period: the simple view of growth as a type of vending machine suggested by a superficial reading of the Harrod–Domar formula, i.e. that you put in more savings and investment and you pull out more growth, had given way to an understanding that even growth, let alone development, is a much more complex process, and that in particular it involves factors relating to human rather than physical capital. So in this respect it was particularly important that the golden years showed rapid progress, not only in physical investment rates, but also in such indicators of human capital formation as spreading literacy and education, elimination of a number of diseases, and reduced mortality rates, including infant mortality rates. This progress in human indicators could be shown to be only tenuously related to GNP growth, illustrating both the limitations of 'trickle down' and the possibility of development along alternative routes.

But since all this encouraging progress was made in a period of rapid growth in the industrial countries and a situation in these countries, as a result of full employment and the Keynesian consensus, extremely favourable to trade liberalization, it was not clear during the golden years to what extent the growth achieved was dependent on the existence of an 'engine of growth' outside the control of the developing countries themselves. This was to be tested when the favourable international climate was drastically changed in the early years of the following decade of the 1970s, signifying the end of the golden years period. It was then that the lack of an internal dynamism in many countries, due often to neglect of agriculture and of indigenous technological capacity, became painfully apparent.

4. The 1970s: Growth Maintained? The Illusion of Debt-led Growth

The decade of the 1970s saw the breakdown and disintegration of the Bretton Woods system. The best date to attach to the end of Bretton Woods is probably 15 August 1971 when President Nixon suspended the free convertibility of the US dollar into gold at the fixed rate agreed at Bretton Woods. This ended the era of fixed exchange rates and destroyed the foundations of even the truncated Bretton Woods which had emerged. The breakdown of the system was more immediately connected with the emerging payment imbalances between the industrial countries, but also with increasing concerns with 'overheating' of their economies and a consequent displacement of full employment by control of inflation as a priority objective. Thus the engine of growth which had supported the developing countries during the golden era began to stutter and then violently change gear. But the event which most marked the 1970s and gave a disarrayed international system its final ominous push was the assertion of oil power by OPEC in 1973–74, with the decade suitably ending with a second assertion of oil power in 1979–80. This provided an opportunity for broader assertion of commodity power and for fundamental shifts in international economic relations; in the event, however, this opportunity was not realized.

So here again we can speak of 'a splendid story not wholly true'. The splendid part of the story was that if we simply look at growth rates, the developing countries as a whole, and even the oil-importing developing countries, proved quite capable of continuing their growth rates even in the face of reduced growth and serious recessions in the industrial countries. In fact, contrary to what happened during the preceding two decades, the gap in per capita income between the developing countries and the industrial market economies narrowed rather than widened during 1970–81, at least in relative terms.

A MIXED PICTURE

The maintenance of growth during this period is, however, subject to some qualification. The growth rate of GDP for all developing economies, excepting the high-income oil exporters, receded from the high rate of 6 per cent per annum which it had reached during 1965–70, the last five golden years, to 5.2 per cent in 1971–80, although this was still higher than the average figure for the preceding two decades. The serious exception was sub-Saharan African, where the 1971–80 growth rate not only fell much more heavily (from 4.8 to 3.3 per cent), but was lower than at any period during 1950–70. In per capita terms, growth in sub-Saharan Africa was virtually wiped out; 16 out of 41 African countries showed absolute declines. This phenomenon of development in reverse, then still confined to half of sub-Saharan Africa, was to become more widespread in the 1980s. In the three worst cases of declines of over 4 per cent per annum (Angola, Chad and Uganda), this reversal was associated with civil wars, and could thus still be ascribed to 'extra-economic' causes. At the other extreme, the Middle East and North Africa, benefiting directly or indirectly from high oil prices, achieved new growth records, well beyond the level of the two preceding decades, and the East Asia and Pacific region maintained the very high growth rate of 8 per cent which it had achieved in the preceding five years. But Latin America and South Asia shared the African decline, although less drastically: both these regions, accounting for most of the population of developing countries (outside China), more or less returned to the growth rates of the earlier part of the two golden decades.

There was also vigorous progress in the competitive position of developing countries in world trade in manufactures. While absolute levels of imports of manufactures by industrial countries were held down by their slower growth and protectionist measures, the share of developing countries in their total markets and in their total imports increased, although from low levels (from 1.7 per cent of the total market share in 1970 to 3.4 per cent in 1979), with all classes of manufactured goods sharing in the increase. The increase in the share of developing countries in total trade of manufactured goods from 13.5 per cent in 1970 to 16.5 per cent in 1979 was, however, entirely concentrated on Far Eastern countries; Latin America and other regions failed to participate in this increase. Both shares in industrial country and world markets are still quite small and should leave room for further expansion in the light of new comparative advantages, always with the important proviso that protectionist measures in the industrialized countries do not prevent this.

Moreover, the maintained growth of GDP is subject to some doubt concerning the D (for 'domestic'), and this applies specifically to the growth of manufactured exports. We have already seen that during the golden years the expected preponderance of aid and official development assistance over private investment had been reversed. During the 1970s aid from Western countries continued to stagnate and dwindle, well below the modest UN target, while private capital continued to flow strongly, supported both by the maintained 'credit-worthiness' of developing countries bolstered by commercial bank lending of recycled OPEC surpluses, and also by the revolution of communications which made internationalization of operations much easier. As a result, by the mid-1970s in Latin America and Africa, typically 40–50 per cent of manufacturing industry was controlled by foreign firms (in some countries 60–70 per cent). In Asia this share was typically lower (India and South Korea 10–15 per cent) although in some Asian countries the share reached or exceeded 40–50 per cent. In the light of the high share of foreign firms in manufacturing in Latin America and Africa, the conventional warning against an 'enclave' character of foreign investment appears ironical; it was domestic manufacturing control which was beginning to look like an enclave. It was equally ironic that industrialization had been recommended as a way of 'de-linking' from an unequal world economy; in fact, it was leading to firmer integration.

Thus, the cherished aim of industrialization as a means of strengthening national independence had been widely missed. The real growth factor in the 1970s, apart from some oil exporters, had come from neither the industrial nor the developing countries, but from the TNCs (transnational corporations). The typical sales value of the large TNCs had become equal to or higher than the total GDP even of many larger and better-off developing countries. (Exxon, for example, has a sales value equivalent to the GDP of Argentina or Nigeria, close to South Korea, more than twice the GDP of Egypt or Pakistan, and almost four times that of Chile or Peru.) Even the last in ranking of the 20 largest TNCs had sales equal to the GDP of Morocco. To a TNC, investment in any given developing country is usually a small, often marginal, part of its total operations and easily fungible; while to a developing country the operation would be an important, and perhaps technologically indispensable, part of its manufacturing capacity – a situation clearly not making for an equal bargaining position. Competition among TNCs helps to balance the scales, but may be offset, or more than offset, by competition among LDCs for the money and technology of the TNCs.

The data for the import-purchasing power of total exports by developing countries also seem to tell a 'splendid story', but once again further analysis shows it to be not wholly true. In the aggregate, this increased faster between 1970 and 1980 than for industrial countries, but the following points should be borne in mind:

- 1980 represented a peak year for oil export values, and much of this favourable differential had been lost by 1983; for developing countries other than major oil exporters the purchasing power of exports increased more slowly than in industrial countries;

- the aggregate figures do not take into account the more rapid increase in population in developing countries; on a per capita basis the comparison would be less favourable;
- the least developed countries actually showed an absolute decline in the purchasing power of their exports by over 13 per cent;
- even among the remaining countries, the favourable differential was entirely confined to exporters of manufactures; the other countries fell behind the industrial countries, in relative terms.

Another apparent achievement of the 1970s was that the successful assertion of producer power in the case of oil interrupted the deteriorating trend in terms of trade of developing countries as a whole for all primary commodities taken as a whole; though of course, the oil-importing countries had a very different story of sharp deterioration to tell. But taking the developing countries as a whole, the improvement in terms of trade through high oil prices shifted financial surpluses and financial power strongly in the direction of the Third World. This raised great hopes of using this newly found power for the establishment of a new international economic order (NIEO). It also raised the possibility of creating an indigenous dynamic of development within the Third World itself, and the prospect of using the new financial power for the creation of indigenous technological capacity. The sad part of the story is that this opportunity was lost, and the NIEO ran into the sands. Worse, the way the oil surpluses were recycled through EURO dollars and the commercial banks of the industrial countries, as well as the new non-Keynesian deflationary response of the industrial countries, together ensured that the net outcome would be adverse to the Third World. Not only was the opportunity lost, but it turned into a trap: the term 'debt trap' which became current in the 1980s is an apt description of what happened.

But we are concerned here not so much with the history of this decade as with the lessons of experience that were drawn for development policy and for development thinking during this time. In the first place, there was a growing disillusionment with growth as a necessary and sufficient development objective. This was not in any way due to a slowing of actual growth in the course of the golden years. Quite on the contrary, the growth rate of developing countries speeded up from 4.2 per cent in 1950–60 to 5.1 per cent in 1960–65 and 6.0 per cent in 1965–70. Even the growth rate of the low-income countries taken as a whole speeded up during the period, although less than in the middle-income countries, as well as starting from a lower level, so that the gap between the two groups widened over the two decades. Rather, the disillusionment was due to increasing evidence that rapid growth of GNP could be combined with growing unemployment and underemployment, increasing poverty, and often also greater inequality of income distribution. At the same time the industrial countries also became disillusioned with growth, although for rather different reasons, since in their experience growth led to inflationary pressures and balance of payments trouble. For the developing countries the shift in objectives from simple growth initially took two forms: one was the establishment of employment as an overriding objective; the other was a shift to redistribution.

THE NEW EMPLOYMENT PRIORITY

The shift to an emphasis on employment was based on evidence of increasing unemployment and underemployment, both in urban and rural areas. The social and political tensions and pressures thus created were seen to undermine the foundations of continued growth so that there was a need for a new approach. Although there was much talk at that time of a 'dethronement of GNP', this is not a very good description of what happened. Growth continued to be regarded as a necessary condition for development, but was no longer accepted as a sufficient condition. Employment creation was not seen as an alternative to growth, but as a proper instrument of growth which would produce not only growth in itself but also a pattern of growth conducive to more equal income distribution, less poverty, more social contentment and less political unrest. In development analysis, this shift to employment objectives was typified by the move from the Arthur Lewis model, in which the surplus labour released from agriculture was assumed to be more or less fully absorbed by the growing urban industries, to the Harris–Todaro model. Under the Harris–Todaro model the drift to the towns would be far in excess of available employment opportunities; the gap between rural subsistence incomes and wages in the modern industrial urban sector would attract job seekers from the rural areas in a multiple ratio equal to the income gap. If modern urban sector wages are three times rural incomes, one-third of the chance of a job would be sufficient to attract a migrant from the rural areas; hence there would be three job seekers for each available job and two-thirds of them would remain unemployed or condemned to make a living as well as they could in the informal sector. This model seemed to correspond much better to reality than the Arthur Lewis model.

The shift to employment as a main objective was quite logically accompanied by particular emphasis on the need for employment-intensive technologies; so this also became the era of a search for and emphasis on 'appropriate' technologies. Moreover, since small-scale production is normally more employment-intensive than large-scale production, it also became the era of 'small is beautiful'. Equally logically, with employment moving to the centre as the crux of development, such 'human capital' aspects as training, skills, health and other factors in productivity were now given increased weight, compared with physical capital accumulation.

In institutional terms, the new emphasis on employment placed the International Labour Organization (ILO) in the centre of development policy, particularly through its newly organized World Employment Programme. The ILO employment missions, first with 'pilot missions' to Colombia, Sri Lanka and Kenya and subsequently many other countries, had a considerable impact on policy and thinking. This was true in particular of the Kenya Employment Mission, which also marked the transition from an emphasis on employment to an emphasis on the need for a more direct attack on poverty, by pointing out that the so-called unemployment or underemployment in developing countries was a misnomer. In fact, most of the so-called unemployed or underemployed were working quite hard to earn a living; the real problem was their low income levels. They were the 'working poor' rather than the 'unemployed'. The Kenya Mission also drew attention to the potential of the informal sector as a source for the labour-intensive and appropriate technology needs, rather than an undesirable residual as it appeared in the Harris–Todaro model.

The new 'employment-oriented strategy' had some obvious limitations. The idea of labour-intensive small-scale appropriate technology conflicted with the desire for industrialization and modernization; the creation of 'appropriate technology' required a technological capacity in some ways even greater than that required for the earlier growth-oriented investment pattern. The latter could to a large extent be imported or imitated, whereas the appropriate technology would have to be newly created. Ironically, under the Harris–Todaro model, the creation of more employment would only intensify the urban unemployment problem, since for every new job there would be several migrants as long as rural surplus labour was available. Reliance on employment-oriented strategy also conflicted with the increasing role of direct foreign investors and multinational corporations. Also, employment could not deal with the poverty groups not capable of employment: those too old to work, too ill, crippled, broken families, orphaned children, and so on. Employment to provide an income does not solve the problem of access to health, education, clean water, sanitation, and so on – all services which relate to public action rather than employment.

Yet in spite of such limitations, the employment orientation had a valid and lasting impact. It emphasized not only the contribution to production which employment could provide, but also the sense of participation and self-respect which improved earning capacity from employment could bring: the issue of human rights as a development objective emerged at this stage. Employment emphasis was especially useful in the agricultural sector, where the basis for an appropriate technology already existed, and it became increasingly realized that the small-scale farmer was more productive in terms of output per acre than the large farmer, and also was quite capable of responding to economic incentives.

Employment creation in the rural sector also became the key to agricultural improvement through public works schemes, particularly during the slack agricultural seasons, and in times of drought or other emergencies. It was discovered that not only emergencies but also persistent poverty were due not so much to a lack of food available, but rather to a breakdown in the 'entitlement' mechanism for obtaining access to food and other essentials of life. Employment, either for an income or directly paid in food, was perhaps the most obvious way of creating such entitlements.

An employment-oriented development policy also provided an essential bridge between the growth-oriented strategy emphasizing 'productive' investment, and a subsequent poverty orientation which could be accused of shifting to 'unproductive' activities such as redistribution, provision of social services subsidies and direct income support. Employment creation was at the same time clearly productive and yet naturally targeted so as to achieve greater equality of income distribution and produce a better trickle-down effect on the poor than mere growth by itself. Nobody could accuse an employment-oriented strategy of playing 'zero-sum games'.

Where employment creation seemed most successful, as in the case of the East Asian 'tigers', it was because it was nurtured both by a high degree of literacy, education, skill and willingness to train in the labour force, and a rapid development of general technological capacity (rather than a specific 'appropriate technology') which enabled them to remain internationally competitive in labour-intensive lines of export even with rising real wages, and to maintain an equal income distribution. It was such factors, rather than concentration on employment creation as such, which made for expansion of employment – in other words, employment was more of a result than an objective or instrument of policy.

THE REDISTRIBUTION PRIORITY

The other shift in development strategy during the earlier part of the 1970s, apart from the emphasis on employment objectives, was greater concern with income distribution, or 'Redistribution With Growth' (RWG). This was, of course, linked to employment-oriented strategies: an increase in employment would normally also improve the equality of income distribution, particularly if it related to agriculture, the informal sector and was based on labour-intensive technologies, as proposed. So it is not surprising that the RWG strategy emerged from the Kenya Employment Mission Report, which contained a chapter entitled 'Redistribution From Growth'. The subtle shift from redistribution *from* growth to redistribution *with* growth added an important new element. Redistribution from growth put growth first and then suggested the use of the resources created by growth for deliberate distributive measures, rather than waiting for 'trickle down'. This policy, which could be described as 'incremental income distribution', was put forward as having the great advantage of making redistribution politically more acceptable, since it would come out of additional resources and nobody would be absolutely worse off. This aspect of growth first and redistribution afterwards from the resources created by growth was always a worrying weakness, since it disregarded the possibility, perhaps likelihood, that the policies needed to promote growth might be incompatible with redistributive policies (and vice versa), and hence that one might undermine the other.

The shift to redistribution with growth emphasized the simultaneity and complementarity of redistribution and growth: it was part of the greater emphasis on human capital, with a denial of a trade-off between distribution and growth, and instead an assertion of the compatibility and complementarity of the two. A number of development analysts went one step further and advocated redistribution *before* growth. An important argument for this was that Japanese and Korean growth, for example, owed both its intensity and egalitarian character to the fact that through land reform, heavy investment in education and health, and so on, physical and human capital assets were fairly equally distributed before the growth process started. It was argued that in this way growth not only had a more solid and sustainable foundation, but would also assume a pattern which was favourable for sustained equality and poverty reduction.

The shift in thinking away from growth towards employment and redistribution in the early 1970s found a particularly ready echo in the World Bank which at that time (the McNamara period) had a liberal phase (in the sense of Keynesian/progressive) in sharp contrast to its subsequent domination by monetarist and neo-liberal views (this time in the Chicago sense). The World Bank became a lead agency in advocating RWG strategies, emphasizing the importance of human capital investment and helping to promote directly poverty-oriented 'basic needs strategies'. One indication of the compatibility of these strategies with growth was that the World Bank's rate of return on its projects did not suffer in this period.

This shift also had implications for approaches to development planning. The original stress on GNP growth focuses attention on macroeconomic planning, which indeed was developed in close parallel with implementing GNP targets. This is less true of employment targets. Clearly there is no single homogeneous employment problem; the problem of the unemployed school leaver, for example, is rather different from that of the small farmer without access to water. So an employment emphasis paves the way for a less aggregated and more dispersed view of planning. This is even more true as we move to poverty and basic needs objectives. The character of the different poverty groups is even more diverse and heterogeneous than the different employment problems. Moreover, the nature of poverty problems may vary even among neighbouring villages, or among urban households living close to each other in the same town. Thus poverty-oriented planning and the provision of basic requirements for population groups now lacking them are by their very nature, and almost by definition, a highly decentralized affair. Local planning as well as local participation, particularly on the part of those directly affected by the lack of basic requirements, are naturally moving into the foreground of the picture. Community development, rather than central planning, seems the natural principal tool of a basic needs-oriented development strategy.

Perhaps ironically, this particular implication of RWG/basic needs strategies, in moving away from the centralized macroeconomic planning associated with GNP growth to looser and more decentralized approaches, was to fit in well with criticism of centralized planning coming from quite a different direction during the tide of neo-liberal counter-revolution characteristic of the 1980s.

The lower growth rate and re-emergence of unemployment in the industrial countries almost inevitably meant an increase in their protectionism. The attempts by GATT to reduce tariffs and liberalize trade were more than offset by increased non-tariff barriers, 'voluntary' export restraints, further tightening up of agricultural policies with inevitable protectionist consequences, and other ways of evading the spirit – if not the letter – of GATT. These non-tariff barriers applied with greater severity to developing countries than to North–North trade, and affected about a quarter of their total exports. The protectionist measures already introduced against an export thrust from a limited number of developing countries give some indication of the industrialized countries' possible response if a more widespread competitive export expansion were attempted.

In addition to rising protectionism, the abandonment of fixed, or at any rate stable, exchange rates in favour of floating rates introduced new elements of uncertainty into the international trade prospects of developing countries. Under normal circumstances such uncertainty would have been an argument for greater inward orientation, reliance on import substitution and expansion of trade of developing countries among themselves. If this did not happen to any significant degree, it was largely because the pressures on import capacity deriving from industrial countries' protectionism and from trade uncertainties were swamped by the readiness, indeed the passionate keenness, of commercial banks in the big financial centres to offer loans, initially at low or negative real rates of interest. This made it relatively easy to maintain imports, even in the face of more precarious export prospects and uncertainties. The temptation for developing countries to avoid timely adjustment to the less favourable climate of the 1970s by relying on 'easy money' from the commercial banks, offered not only readily but without conditions, proved too much to resist. This overall picture did not apply equally to all developing countries; the four East Asian tigers, for example, showed their remarkable capacity for adjustment by absorbing high oil prices, increasing protectionist barriers for their exports and countering exchange rate uncertainties by raising productivity, keeping real wages low and demonstrating a strong planning capacity in picking winners. Moreover, they did this with less reliance on commercial bank loans than the Latin American countries.

Another factor which maintained the growth of countries like South Korea, but also a number of other developing countries, was the spill-over effect of OPEC surpluses. OPEC aid and investment programmes were developed, although aid was highly concentrated in Middle Eastern countries and investment often channelled through the financial institutions of industrial countries. But additional exports to oil exporters, the export of labour to these countries resulting in significant remittances back to the developing home countries, as well as the procurement of construction and other contracts in oil-rich countries, all helped to maintain growth. Although this was a more solid basis than borrowing from commercial banks, in that it did not result in an increased debt burden, it also turned out to be a somewhat precarious and temporary source of development finance, dependent on the continuance of the large OPEC surpluses. It was still 'dependent development', although from the point of view of the Third World as a whole it could be considered as a better approach to self-reliance. But in the event, the OPEC engine of growth proved as temporary as the Keynesian growth of the industrial countries during the golden years had been, and the opportunities it offered were not taken. Instead of laying new foundations for sustainable growth in the 1980s, the OPEC engine merely served to replace the failing other engine and postpone the impact of its failure.

THE BREAKDOWN OF BRETTON WOODS – DIVERGENT PERCEPTIONS

The nature of the 1970s as a period of illusionary debt-led growth raises a number of issues which contain important lessons for the future. The initial collapse of the Bretton Woods system in 1971 and the subsequent failure of the industrial countries to coordinate their own exchange rate and other policies, together with the shock in 1973–74 of the first large rise in oil prices, clearly led to quite different perceptions on the part of the industrial and developing countries respectively. The industrial countries at first assumed that the crisis was merely a temporary phenomenon, no doubt a serious hiccup in the progress of the two previous decades but one that could be dealt with through existing institutions, largely by way of normal lending operations of their own commercial banks recycling OPEC surpluses. Meanwhile, the rapid growth with full employment of the golden years might have to be abandoned in favour of slower growth, unemployment and recessionary periods. But at a time when prevailing politics and ideologies were beginning to swing to the right, and the fight against inflation became a chief objective, this price seemed worth paying. In the event the basic assumption that the shift in financial power relations towards developing countries, or at least towards OPEC countries, could be counteracted by the industrial countries turned out to be justified. This perception on the part of the industrial countries further implied that any later debt repayment phase could be easily handled in traditional ways through the resumed growth in the 1980s which was confidently expected, and/or through continued lending and capital transfers. It took the second big rise in oil prices in 1979–80 to shake this view.

On the part of the developing countries there was a different perception. It was felt that the shift in financial power and the successful assertion of commodity power represented a permanent and fundamental break with the past, both necessitating and making possible a new international economic order. The developing countries felt strong enough to confront the industrial countries with programmes and demands for such an order. They underestimated the ability of the industrial countries to absorb the shocks of the early 1970s within the framework of the existing order and institutions, and also their readiness to abandon the Keynesian full employment consensus of the 1950s and 1960s. The lesson of the past had been that it took a crisis of the dimensions of the recession of the 1930s and the World War to create the preconditions for a completely new international order, and even then (as we have seen) there was in the end hesitation and difficulty in adopting wholly new and radical ideas. The developing countries assumed that the upheavals of 1971 and 1973–74 constituted a similar crisis offering a similar opportunity.

In the event, the breakdown of Bretton Woods in 1971 and the assertion of oil power in 1973–74 constituted a crisis sufficient to terminate the progress of the golden years, but not to create a consensus for a new order. By the time the second big oil shock came at the end of the decade, the world system had adjusted to running at a slower rate, and the industrial countries had brought into play their technological capacity to reduce the impact of high oil prices by energy substitution and by changing the volume and pattern of their production, stepping up exploration and new supplies, and so on. Thus, although the recession following the second oil shock was at least as severe as the one after the first oil shock, it once again failed to reach the dimensions required for a consensus on a need for fundamental changes.

With the benefit of hindsight, the developing countries, rather than relying on a perceived fundamental power shift and confronting the industrial countries with a programme for a new order, could have chosen two other strategies. One was to use their new financial power for the creation of a separate international system, at the same time additional to, and partially de-linked from, North–South relations. This was, of course, the route of extended South–South cooperation for which there was in any case plenty of economic scope and justification. Another strategy was to use the power shift which had undoubtedly occurred in the early 1970s to press for more piecemeal concessions and modifications of the battered Bretton Woods system – perhaps restoring some of the missing pieces discussed above – in the hope of inducing the industrial countries to return to the Keynesian consensus of high growth rates and full employment which had stood the developing countries in good stead.

The lesson of events of the 1970s for the developing countries was that assertion of commodity power without control of financial institutions, and not backed up by technological power, is empty and temporary. The same failure was also demonstrated for the assertion of power by individual countries or groups of producers without a system of full collaboration within the Third World as a whole.

5. The 1980s: the Lost Decade – Development in Reverse?

The idea of the 1980s as a decade 'lost' for development could be described as 'a sad story not wholly true'. It is not wholly true most obviously in the geographical sense: the decade may be 'lost' for Latin America, Africa and also the oil exporters (at least compared with the position they achieved in the 1970s) but it is not true of Asia. Given the demographic and economic importance of Asia, it is not clear which is the exception and which is the rule! But for the other three categories mentioned, to speak of a 'lost' decade may be an understatement; for sub-Saharan Africa, in particular, the 1980s became a disastrous decade, and this sub-continent rapidly acquired the character of a marginalized fourth world, increasingly recognized as requiring special action and special criteria. The other true part of this sad story is that the decade was 'lost' to development in that attention shifted to debt settlement, stabilization, adjustment, structural change, liberalization, and so on – often at the expense of everything that had previously been understood as development, whether growth, employment, redistribution, basic needs or reduction of poverty. This shift was associated with the ascent of neo-liberal ideologies, a shift in decision making on development strategy to creditors, donors and international financial institutions, and within the Bretton Woods system from the World Bank, which had traditionally stood for development, to the IMF which had come to stand for 'stabilization'. Perhaps the most symbolic development was the World Bank's shift out of exclusive project lending – previously put forward as the soundest form of development assistance – to balance of payments support in the form of structural adjustment lending and the establishment of a largely IMF-determined 'cross-conditionality' for World Bank action.

The geographical separation between Asia, where development continued, and the rest of the developing world where it was 'lost', had already been foreshadowed in the 1970s. In that period (1969–78) the export volume of Asia (without the Middle East) had increased faster than import volume (10.8 per cent per annum against 8.6 per cent), thus simultaneously constraining debt accumulation and strengthening repayment capacity, while in sub-Saharan Africa and Latin America export volumes increased much slower than import volumes, with the opposite effect. In sub-Saharan Africa, export volume increased by only 1.4 per cent per annum, less than the rate of population increase; even an increase in import volume three times higher at 4.1 per cent was barely sufficient to maintain per capita imports. In Latin America also, import volumes grew over three times more than export volumes (6.4 per cent against 1.7 per cent). The roots of a debt crisis were thus clearly planted in Latin America and Africa, rather than Asia.

For these countries, the 1980s proved a time of rude awakening from the illusionary growth of the 1970s. Over the five years 1982–86 the cumulative percentage falls in per capita GNP totalled 16.5 per cent for sub-Saharan Africa, 9.7 per cent for the highly indebted countries and 11.5 per cent for oil exporters. For all these categories of developing countries this amounted to a major reversal of development, not just a 'lost decade'. The share of industry in GDP in developing countries, which had increased during 1965–80 to that of the industrial market economies, fell back, and by 1986 was again below that of the industrial countries; it was the developing, not the industrial economies which 'de-industrialized'. In sub-Saharan Africa, de-industrialization was precipitous and brought the share of industry below what it had been in 1970; industrial output declined absolutely by 2.3 per cent per annum during the first half of the decade. There were also absolute declines in the highly indebted countries and the high-income oil exporters. Investment ratios generally declined for practically all categories of developing countries; in the aggregate, the fall from 26.9 per cent of GDP in 1980 to 23.5 per cent in 1986 brought the ratio below the 1973 level; again the cuts in the ratio were sharpest in sub-Saharan Africa and in the highly indebted countries; thus again the focus of development reversal emerges clearly. The terms of trade of developing countries as a whole deteriorated during 1981–86 by a cumulative percentage of 13.9 (but 34.1 for sub-Saharan Africa and 17.3 for the highly indebted countries). The only thing that seemed to be vigorously increasing for many categories of developing countries was their outstanding debt, with debt service reaching 4.3 per cent of GNP and absorbing 19.7 per cent of exports (as much as 29.6 per cent in sub-Saharan Africa and 27.8 per cent in the highly indebted countries). External debts in 1987 exceeded three years' exports for both sub-Saharan Africa and the 15 heavily indebted countries. The main exception of Asia must be re-emphasized. The overall performance of low-income countries was held up by the remarkable progress of China and India, which dominate this category, and exporters of manufactures were buttressed by the success stories of the East and South-East Asian NICs. Predictably, during the decade much debate centred around the lessons from Asian successes and the ways in which they could be transplanted to Africa and other parts of the developing world.

The 1980s opened with a strong recession which represented a culminating point of the contest between commodity power on the one hand, and technological and financial power on the other. Commodity power was represented by the second quadrupling of oil prices in 1979–80, while the technological and financial power of the industrial countries was represented by their capacity to reduce the oil content of production, to step up oil exploration and substitution for oil, and to reduce the demand for oil further by accepting or even welcoming a recession which would reduce inflation as well as the demand for oil. In this contest, technological/financial power proved to be stronger than commodity power, all the more so since the industrial countries had had the chance of adjusting to higher oil prices seven years earlier, when they first quadrupled in 1973–74.

For the oil-importing developing countries the constellation of circumstances could not have been worse. These were:

- reduced import volumes by the developing countries with recession and protectionism interacting in the same direction;
- highly unfavourable terms of trade, as a result both of high oil prices and a deterioration of other commodity prices in relation to their manufactured imports from industrial countries (the latter increased by high energy costs);
- a reduction and, later, virtual cessation of commercial bank lending and a rise in real interest rates so that debt burdens were increased both through lower export earnings and higher service payments simultaneously;
- a strong appreciation of the dollar in the early years of the decade resulting from the high rates of interest;
- spreading 'aid fatigue' among industrial countries due to both the recession and the spread of monetarist neo-liberal ideologies.

The shortcomings of the Bretton Woods system in providing no mechanism for the industrial countries and the balance of payments surplus countries to recover made themselves strongly felt. All these circumstances conspired to make the 1980s a lost decade for development. It was a sign of the times that even under such conditions it could be seriously debated whether the internal policies of developing countries, rather than external circumstances, were responsible for their difficulties.

Yet just at a time when the international climate became so disastrously hostile to development, the bastions of financial power in the industrial countries and in the leading financial institutions were captured by a neo-liberal ideology which preached all-out 'outward orientation' and 'market orientation' as the secret of successful development. If the 1950s and 1960s could be said to have displayed a time-lagged misplaced trade pessimism based on prewar experience, so the 1980s could be said to be dominated by a doctrinal and time-lagged trade optimism based on the trade expansion of the 1950s and 1960s and the subsequent illusionary maintenance of developing country imports in the 1970s. The crucial difference, however, was that the inward-oriented industrialization policies of the 1950s and 1960s were almost certainly justified as a necessary foundation for a subsequent successful outward orientation in a favourable economic climate; whereas the policies now impressed on developing countries under the name of outward orientation were intended not to lay the foundations for subsequent sustainable growth (although that was their supposed purpose), but rather to permit payment of their debts.

Here again there was a tragic time lag. Adjustment and restructuring for the purpose of repaying debts – or rather of keeping debts within more manageable limits – would have been an appropriate requirement for the 1970s. The maintenance of import capacity at the expense of balance of payments deficits and increasing indebtedness could have been justified only if the policies of the developing countries had then been firmly directed towards using the borrowed capital to build up a firm position in tradables permitting a discharge of debt service. Given the inability of industrial countries to prevent the slowed-down growth and sporadic recessions of the 1970s, or even their willingness to repeat such recessions and accept unemployment as part of their fight against inflation and OPEC power, the developing countries during the 1970s would have had to rely as much, or more, on import substitution than on export promotion. That at least would be an overall judgement, without excluding the possibility of specific countries finding their place in a pattern of a gradual increase in the capacity of a number of developing countries to export manufactures of a genuinely national character, i.e. other than as a result of relocation and internationalization of production on the part of the transnational corporations.

To the extent that this did not happen, there is an element of truth in holding the domestic policies of developing countries responsible for some of the troubles of the 1980s. This, however, is subject to some significant qualifications: at the time, in the 1970s, when exhortations to restructure in preparation for debt settlement would have been appropriate, not much was heard in this direction from those now in a position not only to advise but to impose such policies. Instead, the developing countries were encouraged to borrow without conditionality or much control of the use of the borrowed resources. Moreover, the type of internal policy that would have been needed in the 1970s was not the type of structural adjustment advocated in the 1980s. There is no evidence that the rise in real interest rates and the severe global recession of the early 1980s was foreseen at the time of low or negative rates in the 1970s.

The policies now impressed upon developing countries under the signs of restructuring, adjustment, retrenchment, stabilization and so on are justified on the grounds that they are necessary to 'lay the foundations of subsequent sustainable growth'. Leaving aside the question of symmetrical adjustment required from industrial, creditor and balance of payments surplus countries, this approach disregards one of the basic insights of the early development period of the 1950s. Much thinking prevalent then had been based on a view of development and growth as a process of 'cumulative causation', or a system of (beneficial or vicious) circles or spirals. The vicious circle of poverty, for example, was well established: poor people are poor because they are undernourished or illiterate, and they are undernourished and illiterate because they are poor. In the same way, poor countries are poor because they have low savings and investment and they have low savings and investment because they are poor. In the strategy of balanced growth, the vicious circle took the form of treating the failure of section A to grow as due to the failure of other sectors B, C, D, and so on to grow and supply both the inputs and demand for sector A; the same is true of sector B, which fails to grow because sector A fails to grow. In the 'stages of growth' paradigm developed by Rostow this took the form of saying that the earlier stages of assembling the preconditions for growth are very difficult, but once the various elements have been assembled and can mutually complement each other, everything will fall into place and the economy can take off.

The present doctrine of neo-liberal adjustment is in danger of disregarding all this. It holds that one can temporarily deflate, arrest growth, reduce government expenditures, reduce expenditures on physical and human investments and so on, while at the same time gathering strength for a new and, it is hoped, more sustainable period of growth and development. This disregards the possibility that each cutback may make it more difficult to resume future growth from such a weakened basis. The picture of a 'slippery slope' may be more appropriate than the picture of *reculer pour mieux sauter* (stepping back to gain room for a forward jump) which underlies the neo-liberal approach to adjustment. Yet this possibility is not sufficiently considered or guarded against in the climate of the 1980s.

Yet the neo-liberal critics of earlier development policies deserve to be listened to seriously. It had become apparent to the developing countries themselves that a regime of overvalued exchange rates carried dangers of inefficient allocation, rent seeking, capital flight and so on; that prices and markets have a role to play in the efficient allocation of resources and are often better instruments than administrative regulation or controls; that over-expansion of the government sector might conceivably suppress latent entrepreneurial sources in the private sector which could be released by less regulation; that planning machinery can easily become overcentralized at the expense of local initiative and popular participation; that trade liberalization can be to the advantage of developing countries themselves; that proper price incentives to farmers can be a useful tool for stimulating domestic food production when they can be combined with other measures of a more structural character which are also needed; that industrialization which is at the expense of agriculture can be self-defeating, and should be replaced by a type of development in which agricultural development and industrialization can mutually support each other; that policies should not be excessively 'urban biased'; that subsidies and other measures targeted at lower-income groups often have a way of failing to reach the poorest and sometimes benefit the better-off instead; that public services no less than the private sector should be governed by principles of efficiency and low-cost services, etc. All this long list of insights (which could easily be further extended) had already emerged from previous developments, and there is no need to create a neo-liberal counter-revolution for discovering them. All the same, in so far as the critics of previous strategies have kept on hammering away at these and other shortcomings, they have rendered a useful service. But they have rendered no service by combining these insights with an abandonment of development objectives for the sake of adjustment; by being indifferent to the social impact or 'human face' aspects of the policies they propose; by a failure to put equivalent pressure on surplus countries as well as deficit countries, or on high-income deficit countries as well as poorer deficit countries; by applying doctrines on the value of free markets developed in different circumstances to other circumstances where the assumed conditions simply do not exist; by elevating discharge of debt service to an ultimate objective and allowing it to displace the old consensus objectives of growth, employment, redistribution and basic needs.

The insistence on structural adjustment as a precondition for new development is justified on the grounds that it is not a policy imposed by the international financial institutions and big industrial governments, but rather an inescapable necessity, given the 'facts of life' – these being slower growth in the industrial countries, failure of industrial countries to coordinate balance of payments and exchange rate policies, protectionism, the overhanging debt burden, weakness of commodity prices and so on. This is an argument which is obviously true as far as it goes. Given an international climate so unfavourable to development, the developing countries have no choice but to adjust themselves to it and if necessary cut back their ambitions, and they must try as much as possible to make a virtue of necessity. However, the argument leaves scope for two substantial doubts. First, in the spirit of Bretton Woods and numerous UN resolutions and other proclamations as well as under their own constitutions, it should be the duty of the international financial institutions as well as governments not simply to accept the unfavourable international climate and expect the developing countries to adjust to it, but rather to change and improve it. Second, even if the unfavourable climate is taken as given, it does not follow that the only or even the best form of adjustment is in the nature of 'stabilization', which tends to become a code word for retrenchment. Are there not more expansionary forms of adjustment available? In particular, adjustment through intensified trade and other forms of economic cooperation between developing countries is not included in the adjustment packages now presented. Moreover, the country-by-country approach in which individual, although in essence very similar, packages are imposed country by country seems designed, by its very nature, to set developing countries against each other, for example in trying to expand exports simultaneously. This can be self-defeating due to the fallacy of composition and the possibility of immiserizing growth. The route through increased cooperation among developing countries would often seem more hopeful, but it is not taken up in the dominant neo-liberal approach.

The potential for trade between developing countries remains largely untapped. Expanded South–South trade can be treated as a partial de-linking from the slowed-down rate of growth of the industrial countries no longer acting as an efficient engine of growth, as Arthur Lewis did in his Nobel Prize lecture of 1980. Alternatively, expanded South–South trade can also be supported by those in favour of closer international integration as a stepping stone towards fuller integration on more equal terms. This debate is as fruitless or inconclusive as the question whether a half-filled glass of water is 'half full' or 'half empty'! South–South trade is not the only method open to developing countries to maintain their own growth in a less favourable international climate; other methods include the export-led route in securing a greater share of domestic markets in industrial countries, or successful import substitution, or the development of internal dynamism based on increased technological capacity so as to create a domestic engine of growth to replace the faltering external engine. The latter would almost certainly be required in any case, even for a successful implementation of the other methods of export promotion, import substitution or increased South–South trade. South–South trade in turn can be helpful in creating technological dynamism, and also in providing a basis for improved exports to industrial countries as well as efficient import substitution.

At present only around a quarter of LDC exports go to other developing countries. Thus a given percentage fall in exports to industrial countries would require a three-fold proportionate increase in South–South trade to compensate. However, the heavy taxation of normal export proceeds for debt payment puts a strong premium on unorthodox methods of trade expansion through barter trade, countertrade and so on; South–South trade could play an especially important role in promoting such unorthodox methods of trade expansion.

What is striking is the self-assurance and disregard of institutional specificities with which the neo-liberal recipe is applied by its advocates, in the face of much previous experience, much professional doubt and obvious economic, social and political realities. In this respect, it resembles more a brand of religious fundamentalism than a school of thought. Perhaps this also explains the surprising ease with which this counter-revolution has captured the commanding heights in the dominant countries and institutions. The severe depression of the early 1980s was sufficient to produce fundamental changes, if not in the actual international order then at least in thinking about development. But it is difficult to believe that this shift in thinking will be more lasting than some of the earlier shifts described. Like the other changes in thinking which come and go, and yet leave some of their insights behind, the 'adjustment' period and the neo-liberal religion may have passed its peak in the mid-1980s. There is an increasingly visible wish now, at the beginning of the 1990s, to return to the business of development, which remains a global priority. There is now more doubt about the social, political and environmental consequences of adjustment policies; less self-confidence in the neo-liberal conditionality as against the judgement of LDC governments and many practitioners; less assertion of the doctrine that development is constrained by domestic mismanagement to the exclusion of external factors.

Both physical investment and human capital formation have received serious setbacks during this phase, when concern with development and growth has been largely displaced by adjustment and stabilization. The decline in investment in low-income economies other than China and India, and among major debtor countries and oil exporters, has been described at the beginning of this chapter. Similarly, human capital has been run down alarmingly. As documented by the UNICEF studies on 'Adjustment With a Human Face' and 'The Impact of the World Recession on Children' (Cornia et al., 1987) the cuts in government expenditures have affected the welfare of poorer people and particularly women and children disproportionately; the measures taken under the neo-liberal prescription for adjustment, such as abolition of food subsidies, devaluation, trade liberalization, privatization and so on, have contributed to greater inequalities of income distribution, with the well-to-do in a better position to protect their interests. The resulting deteriorating indicators of child nutrition, child health and schooling, as well as the rise of child mortality – the ultimate indicator – are particularly ominous since their impact on development is bound to be felt for at least a generation. It is difficult to see how this can possibly be described as 'laying the foundations for subsequent substainable growth'.

It is not only growth which has gone into reverse, at least in Africa and Latin America, but also the basic needs strategies of the late 1970s and redistribution (with or without growth), together with the increase in the savings and investment rations. Thus it may be said that all the previous approaches and recipes for development have been submerged by the new orthodoxy of primacy for coming to terms with the debt crisis, and of conforming to the deterioration of the international climate since the early 1970s.

As the 1980s drew to a close and the broad decline of investment, physical and human, and widespread reversal of development has become apparent, resistance to the neo-liberal counter-revolution has increased. It is now accepted that:

- adjustment has not been sufficiently 'growth-oriented';
- adjustment must be given a more 'human face';
- more external resources are needed to smooth the process of adjustment and make it politically possible;
- adjustment must be made less harsh and stretched out over a longer period;
- some element of debt relief is inevitable as part of the adjustment process;
- the reverse transfers of capital from developing to industrial countries, including even to the international financial institutions, are counter-productive and perverse as well as reverse;
- the neo-liberal recipe is of doubtful validity in an unfavourable economic climate and when applied to low-income countries with difficult structural problems;
- a common ideology (neo-liberal in this case) results in adjustment programmes which are much too similar – almost identical – between different countries and which fail to take sufficient account of country-specific features;
- adjustment must become more symmetrical between debtor and creditor countries, surplus and deficit countries and also between LDC deficit/debtor countries and key currency deficit/debtor countries like the USA.

The adjustment problems which many of the developing countries have faced in the 1980s are unique in their abruptness and cumulative impact. The problem is at least three-fold: first, to adjust to a growth rate of industrial countries which has now been set for 15 years at a 'good year' maximum standard of 3 per cent per annum instead of 5 to 6 per cent of the golden years, and this with interruptions by recessions, without any apparent sign of a return to former growth rates. Second, to deal with the steep deterioration in terms of trade for primary commodity exporters (now also including the oil exporters) which brought commodity prices in 1987 to their lowest real level since the 1930s, leaving a major cumulative deterioration by over 40 per cent in terms of trade since 1979. Third, there is the cessation of capital inflows and their replacement by a reverse transfer of capital – some of this represented by the capital flight almost inevitably connected with the adjustment plight of developing countries and representing one way in which the well-to-do can protect themselves.

To put this in concrete and broad quantitative terms: developing countries' export earnings are by now perhaps 25–30 per cent lower than they would be if the industrial countries had maintained earlier growth rates and continued trade liberalization. A further tax of perhaps another 30 per cent is put on export earnings as a result of deteriorating terms of trade reducing the import capacity represented by export earnings. Yet another 30 per cent or so represents a tax on export earnings as a result of debt service commitments. For the large number of developing countries simultaneously affected by all three factors, the cumulative tax on export earnings and import capacity represented would be of the total order of around 60–70 per cent, amounting to a real collapse of export earnings available for the financing of developmental imports.

Admittedly, not all countries are simultaneously and equally affected by all three factors; the 25–30 per cent tax on export earnings for debt service in particular is often unsustainable, and leads to reschedulings and increasingly also to measures of debt relief. It is difficult to translate this into the golden years' metaphor of the 'take-off'; the more appropriate metaphor now would be the aborted take-off with heavy damage to the machine which may take quite some time to repair, or even the crash landing. For those parts of the developing world where development has been reversed in the 1980s, perhaps the 1990s will have to be a 'decade of rehabilitation', aided, it is hoped, by a better international climate and a truly international structural adjustment in global relations.

Summing up the experience of the last two decades, we can now see that in some senses all those involved seemed to act rationally in their own interests: the OPEC members in raising the price of oil; the international banks in lending the deposited receipts to then fast-growing third world economies – the very term 'developing countries' suggested a potential for rapid growth. For the developing countries, the chance to borrow funds at low or negative real rates of interest, without conditionality, was too good to miss.

The lack of any appropriate international institutions prevented proper co-ordination of this process. Any desire amongst OPEC members to channel their resources into development projects was heavily circumscribed by a lack of appropriate development agencies. Depositing their funds with commercial banks ensured that they went predominantly to the middle-income developing countries. Furthermore this meant that they flowed in a haphazard way determined by short-term outlooks, rather than a longer-term assessment of LDCs' needs and absorptive capacities that an effective international institution might have provided.

The failings of this process are now all too apparent; in its own way it is a striking example of the severe shortcomings of leaving the distribution of development funds to the free market. Just at the time when the institutions – actual and projected – of Bretton Woods were most needed, they were either disintegrating or surrendering to an ideology which made them agents of retrenchment rather than development – a new policy of NRNG (neither redistribution nor growth), of adjustment without a human face. The 'decade of rehabilitation' will also have to apply to the international system and to international institutions. Some of this rehabilitation will have to consist of retrieving earlier insights and initiatives which we have lost; another part will have to consist of new insights and initiatives. Fortunately, the signs are that the need for this rehabilitation is now too obvious to be disregarded. The road of the 1990s may lead us away from NRNG through AWHF (adjustment with a human face) to a resumed RWG (redistribution with growth) and on to a real Bretton Woods – which is where we came in. The need and prospects for this will be further explored in the last part of the book.

This first part, dealing with general problems rather than those of specific countries, has inevitably put much weight on the international environment which is largely common to developing countries, rather than domestic policies and domestic governance. Any such over-emphasis on the external factors will be rectified in the case studies of Nigeria and India which follow. There is a lively debate whether the external or internal factors are more important. This is really a non-question which cannot be answered in this form – certainly not in any quantitative sense. In this debate, the developing countries tend to emphasize the importance of external factors while the industrial countries put heavy emphasis on domestic governance.

Those who proclaim the dominant importance of domestic factors point to the very divergent records of different developing countries, even though they are faced with the same or similar international environment. They also argue that the developing countries must take the international environment given as a 'fact of life', and that hence it is fruitless for them to keep on moaning about the international environment. The counter-argument emphasizes that the international environment is not a given 'fact of life' to which developing countries must unilaterally adjust, and that institutions like the IMF, World Bank, and United Nations were created to change the external 'facts of life'. Moreover – so the counter-argument continues – if some developing countries manage to do well in spite of an unfavourable external environment, this means that others will be prevented from doing so (the fallacy of composition); whereas in a favourable environment developing countries could move forward together as they roughly did in the golden age.

We shall come back to this debate in the last part of this book. There is clearly merit on both sides of the argument and our conclusion from the case studies will be that sustainable development will involve both action on the international front as well as improved domestic governance.

PART 2

Case Studies

6. Introduction

Part 1 centred on development experience at the global level with emphasis on the external environment, placed in a historical timeframe of three linked periods. Part 2 restores the balance by concentrating on the domestic level, within the same historical frame. It illustrates more fully the thinking, and especially the strategies, discussed in Part 1, using case studies of Nigeria and India, two countries with extensive development experience. This is supported by describing the policies applied to industrial and agricultural sectors, supplemented by poverty and employment programmes, to stimulate growth and reduce poverty. The lessons from the case studies focus on the need for action both on the external and the domestic front to bring about sustainable development.

7.   A Case Study of Nigeria

THE THEME

The central theme is the interaction between the global and the domestic economy, with export-led growth, initially based on agricultural cash crops and subsequently on oil, as a major strategy of development. External conditions, including a boom from rising oil export prices in the 1970s, have been transmitted to the economy, but the capacity to use oil revenues has been heavily influenced by domestic factors. The fall in oil export prices and revenues from the early 1980s, exposed the risks of dependence on a single commodity and the extent to which rising external debts can impinge on development policies.

Development thinking mirrors a shift in emphasis from Keynesian concepts in the golden age and the debt-led growth era to neo-liberal ones in the lost decade, with a belief in state intervention giving way to market forces. These approaches have moulded development strategies, in both industrial and agricultural sectors, to accomplish goals including growth, distribution and debt repayment. The limits of import substitution for heavy industrialization against a weak technological base and inadequacy of food production emerge. Lack of poverty-oriented and employment-based programmes inhibit reduction of inequality and satisfaction of basic needs.

This section highlights economic progress in Nigeria in the postwar period including rates of growth, sectoral structure and exports.[1]

Trade has been prominent in the economy although its importance has been reduced somewhat in recent years, following the collapse in oil prices: exports accounted for 31 per cent of GDP in 1980 falling to 22 per cent of GDP in 1988 while imports accounted for 24 per cent of GDP in 1980 falling to 13 per cent of GDP in 1988.

Nigeria's annual average percentage growth rate of total real product over 1960–87 is revealing (See Table 7.1(a)). It includes the pre-oil era (before October 1973), the oil boom era (1973–80) and the subsequent oil 'doom' (after 1981 when the decline in oil export prices started emerging). The annual average percentage growth rate over 1960–70 was 4.4, while over 1970–80 it rose to 5.4: within 1970–80 it was 7.8 over 1970–75, falling to 3.5 over 1975–80. The growth rate over 1980–87 was negative at –1.9. From

Table 7.1(a)   Annual average growth rates of total real product at market prices, 1960–87 (in %)

1960–87	1960–70	1970–80	1970–75	1975–80	1980–87
4.2	4.4	5.4	7.8	3.5	−1.9

(b)   Annual average growth rates of total real product at market prices, 1980–87 (in %)

1980–81	1981–82	1982–83	1983–84	1984–85	1985–86	1986–87
−5.7	−0.2	−6.2	−7.4	7.6	2.3	−4.6

Source: UNCTAD (1988)

Note: Growth rates of real product are generally based on data on GDP at constant market prices (without any adjustment being made for changes in the terms of trade). The weights used in the aggregate figures are base year weights, at 1980 prices (UNCTAD, 1988).

1980–81 onwards the annual growth rates fluctuated and were usually negative, excepting 1984–85 and 1985–86 (Table 7.1(b)). Recent data based on World Bank statistics suggest that the real growth of GDP in Nigeria was 3.9 per cent in 1988 and 4.9 per cent in 1989. However, a great deal of the improvements in the economies both of Nigeria and of other African countries (i.e. those which did not adopt structural adjustment policies) was due to extraneous factors (and in particular better weather and improvement in the world economy, Mosley, 1991).

The actual growth rates in the oil boom period often fell short of planned growth rates. The instability of the growth rate of the economy was prominent over 1975–80. While growth rates of 1.3 per cent and 1.1 per cent were recorded in 1975–76 and 1978–79 respectively, the years 1976–77, 1977–78 and 1979–80 saw impressive growth rates of 8.7 per cent, 7.5 per cent and 8.8 per cent respectively (Federal Republic of Nigeria, 1981, p. 4).

The structure of production in Nigeria shows that there were considerable changes in the contribution of some of the key sectors to GDP over 1960–84 but this was propelled by mining, comprising primarily the oil sector, and not by industrialization. Services were important throughout the period. Thus, over 1960–80 there was a sharp reduction in the contribution of agriculture but only a limited increase in manufacturing; mining showed a sharp increase. The contribution of services to GDP increased. Following

Table 7.2　Contribution of sectors to GDP (%)

	1960	1970	1975	1980	1985	1986
Agriculture	64.1	44.6	25.6	20.7	35.0	36.3
Mining	1.2	12.0	22.3	31.0	16.5	12.0
Manufacturing	4.8	7.5	5.6	8.4	10.7	11.5
Construction	4.0	6.3	8.7	7.6	1.8	2.4
Services	25.6	29.0	37.5	31.8	35.3	37.2
Utilities	0.3	0.6	0.3	0.5	0.7	0.6

Source:　Based on W.T. Oshikoya (1990), Table 5, using Federal Office of Statistics, *Annual Abstract of Statistics*, Lagos for various years.

Table 7.3　Structure of production

Distribution of gross domestic product in 1989 (%)

Agriculture	31
Industry	44
Services, etc.	25
	100

Source:　World Bank (1991). Industry includes 'manufacturing' which accounted for 10 per cent of GDP in 1989, and also includes mining.

the fall in oil prices in the third quarter of 1981, the contribution of the sectors in 1986 changes somewhat. The contribution of services, and to some extent that of agriculture, rose (Tables 7.2 and 7.3). This pattern has tended to be retained in recent years (Table 7.3). Thus, despite the oil boom, agriculture continues to be a major sector, with limited industrialization. Nigeria's significant oil revenues in the 1970s and early 1980s have not been used to create a modern industrial economy.

International trade has been instrumental in shaping economic activity in Nigeria since the turn of the century. Trade in primary commodities like palm oil, cocoa, cotton, groundnut and rubber has been the chief means by which the country earned foreign exchange up to the time of political independence in 1960. Sterling reserves built through primary commodity exports in the 1950s enabled her to construct the socioeconomic infrastructure on which she started her post-independence development. Efforts at modernizing the economy can be traced to the heavy importation of raw materials and machinery which fuelled the import-substitution industrialization strategy in the 1960s and 1970s (Umo, 1991, pp. 262–3).

Changes in the commodity composition of trade which started in the 1960s were substantially to alter the structure of the economy. The emergence of petroleum as the key export precipitated the demise of the primary exports but also worsened the precarious external dependence of the economy. Oil exports alone accounted for over 95 per cent of the country's foreign exchange earnings, and import dependence on several key areas like food and raw materials (Umo, 1991).

The vulnerability of the Nigerian economy to global recession and the attendant collapse of the oil market in the 1980s can be directly traced to Nigeria's trade profile. The key problems which have emerged in the foreign trade sector include the accumulation of short-term trade arrears and the associated debt crisis, balance of payments deficits, an overvalued currency, smuggling, and so on (Umo, 1991).

Nigeria's total exports experienced the highest growth rate (27 per cent) in the 1970s and had their worst shortfall (–8.6 per cent) in the first seven years of the 1980s. Exports of mineral fuels were reasonably robust and reached a peak of 50 per cent in the 1960s. Exports of food and live animals declined by 70 per cent in the 1960s and recovered to merely 11 per cent in the 1970s (Table 7.4; Umo, 1991, p. 264).

Aggregate imports increased from Naira 431.7 million in 1960 to Naira 756 million in 1970 and reached their highest peak of Naira 12.6 billion in

Table 7.4   Growth trends of some Nigerian exports, 1960–86

Export categories	Growth trends by periods			
	1960–85	1960–70	1970–80	1981–86
Food and live animals	0.06	–0.70	0.11	0.025
	(7.81)	(–2.70)	(4.52)	(0.775)
Crude materials	–0.09	–0.031	–0.65	–0.179
	(–11.88)	(–2.36)	(–1.78)	(3.96)
Mineral fuels	0.27	0.50	0.32	–0.091
	(11.1)	(4.26)	(8.32)	(–2.66)
Manufactured goods	0.06	0.26	–0.14	–0.25
	(0.38)	(3.0)	(–1.12)	(–1.86)
Total exports	0.17	0.063	0.27	–0.086
	(15.05)	(4.21)	(8.90)	(–2.62)

Source: Umo (1991), Table 10.1.

1981. Since 1981, imports have been declining both absolutely and in relative terms. The trend growth rates for aggregate imports and the major components reveal that in the 1960s and 1970s import growth rates were explosive. The sharp increase (29 per cent) in the 1970s can be accounted for by the heavy import for post-civil war reconstruction activities and the access to oil revenue. The sharp decline in imports since the beginning of the 1980s was a product of economic problems which stemmed from the collapse of oil revenues. In terms of the component import categories two key points emerge: first, food imports registered the highest growth rate (34 per cent) in the 1970s, followed by imports of machinery and transport equipment which accounted for 30 per cent during the same decade. Indeed, the 1970s was an 'age of import boom' in Nigeria. Second, the high import dependency

Table 7.5   Growth trends of some Nigerian imports, 1960–86

Import categories	Growth trends by periods			
	1960–85	1960–70	1970–80	1981–86
Total imports	0.16	0.91	0.29	−0.116
	(12.03)	(0.68)	(9.32)	(−1.55)
Foods and live animals	0.18	−0.026	0.24	
	(12.19)	(−0.63)	(16.13)	
Chemicals	0.16	0.098	0.15	0.068
	(10.51)	(10.84)	(1.83)	(0.48)
Machinery and	0.14	−0.03	0.30	0.165
transport equipment	(5.45)	(−0.20)	(7.79)	(−1.69)

Source: Umo (1991), Table 10.2.

Table 7.6   Terms of trade (1973=100)

1973	100	1980	448.4
1974	292.8	1981	487.9
1975	258.7	1982	452.9
1976	281.1	1983	433.2
1977	287.0	1984	435.4
1978	256.9	1985	396.9
1979	317.0	1986	198.6

Source: Based on Oshikoya, (1990).

of the economy is illustrated by the fact that the average growth rates of different import categories were quite robust including food and animals (18 per cent) chemicals (16 per cent) and machinery and equipment (14 per cent; see Table 7.5 and Umo, 1991, pp. 265–7).

The terms of trade which measures the ratio of export to import prices is one of the most important indicators of external shocks to the economy. Nigeria's terms of trade improved dramatically in 1974 following the increase in oil prices. The terms of trade started to deteriorate from 1982 onwards, in line with the fall in oil prices from the third quarter of 1981 (Table 7.6).

Nigeria has been heavily dependent on exports for her income. Till the early 1970s exports of cash crops provided the bulk of foreign exchange revenues. However, from the early 1970s onwards, oil replaced cash crops, bringing in about 90 per cent of income from exports, and about 80 per cent of government income. Oil prices, oil production and government revenues and foreign exchange inflows increased sharply. There was a sharp fall in the value of these variables from 1981.

Oil price per barrel rose from $3 in 1971 to $11 in 1973. Subsequently, the price rose sharply over 1975–80, although there were fluctuations, with a peak of $44 per barrel in 1980. But oil prices started falling from 1981 onwards (Table 7.7). This hit a low of about $10–$12 per barrel in 1985.

Table 7.7 Production, export, posted price and government revenue from crude oil in Nigeria

Year	Production (million bbl/day)	Export (million bbl/day)	Posted price ($/bbl)	Revenue to government (Naira million)	
1975	1.785	1.713	13.7	4733	(1975–76)
1976	2.067	2.013	14.0	5498	(1976–77)
1977	2.085	2.030	15.5	6177	(1977–78)
1978	1.897	1.827	14.9	4809	(1978–79)
1979	2.302	2.210	33.0	10100	(1979–80)
1980	2.054	1.940	44.0	9489	(Apr–Dec)
1981	1.440	1.227	42.5	9825*	
1982	1.294	0.991	39.0	5161*	

*Estimates

Source: Federal Ministry of National Planning, National Economic Council (1983), using data from Nigerian National Petroleum Corporation and Federal Government Budget Estimates.

Table 7.8   Price of crude petroleum ($/bbl)

1986	(3rd quarter)	12.4	1988	(1st quarter)	15.9
	(4th quarter)	13.8		(2nd quarter)	16.3
1987	(1st quarter)	18.0		(3rd quarter)	14.5
	(2nd quarter)	18.7		(4th quarter)	13.7
	(3rd quarter)	19.2	1989	(1st quarter)	17.9
	(4th quarter)	18.1		(2nd quarter)	19.1
				(3rd quarter)	17.6
				(4th quarter)	19.5

Source: Economist Intelligence Unit (1989).

Although prices increased somewhat from 1986 onwards, they were far below the peak years of 1979 and 1980 (Table 7.8).

Disruption of oil supplies from Iraq, and the threat of a war in the Middle East, led to a short-term increase in the price per barrel to over $30 in the third quarter of 1990 but it fell again to $20 per barrel after peace was restored. In May 1991, oil prices fell below $20 per barrel: taking Nigerian average spot prices it was $18.35 per barrel for medium and $19.45 per barrel for Bonny Light (Economist Intelligence Unit, 1991, p. 17).

Increase and decrease in production of oil for the domestic and the export market accompanied the rise and fall in oil prices (Tables 7.7–7.9).

Inflows of foreign exchange and government revenues have been governed by the behaviour of oil exports (Tables 7.7 and 7.10). Despite a considerable fall in income from oil, Nigeria's imports remained high, with a net outflow of foreign exchange between 1981 and 1983 (Table 7.10). Nigeria was drawing on her reserves to finance imports, marking a phase of 'illusionary growth'.

Table 7.9   Oil production, domestic consumption and exports (in million bbl/day)

	1980	1981	1982	1983	1984	1985	1986	1987	1988
Oil production	2.06	1.44	1.28	1.24	1.39	1.50	1.47	1.29	1.37
Domestic consumption	0.21	0.22	0.27	0.31	0.30	0.25	0.25	0.25	0.25
Net export	1.91	1.23	1.00	0.94	1.09	1.25	1.22	1.04	1.12

Source: World Bank (1988).

Table 7.10   Foreign exchange inflow and outflow (in million Naira)

Year	Inflow	Outflow	Netflow
1970	644	593	51
1971	1039	914	125
1972	1197	1234	−37
1973	2237	1469	769
1974	5313	2186	3127
1975	5491	5517	−26
1976	6581	6901	−321
1977	7743	8281	−538
1978	7607	8991	−1384
1979	10458	8664	1794
1980	14255	11805	2450
1981	11574	14568	−2993
1982	9502	10963	−1461
1983	8364	10921	−2557
1984	8930	8685	245
1985	11024	10463	561
1986	10239	8293	1946

Source: Based on Oshikoya (1990), Table 9, p. 83.

Indebtedness became a major problem from 1982 onwards, and mirrored the collapse in oil prices and production. External debts reached $US12 459 million in 1985, $US16 546 million in 1986 and $US26 057 million in 1987 (UNCTAD, 1988 and World Bank, 1989b). The 1991 budget estimates show that the debt reached $31.5 billion in October 1990 (*Financial Times*, 12 March 1991). Debt servicing increased sharply after 1980 (Table 7.11). In 1989 total external debt as a percentage of GNP was 119.3 in marked contrast to only 9.0 in 1980 (World Bank, 1991, p. 250).

Table 7.11   Debt servicing as percentage of exports of goods and services

1975	4.4	1985	28.9
1980	4.3	1986	23.4
1983	18.1	1989	21.3
1984	25.6		

Source: UNCTAD (1988). Data for 1989 based on World Bank (1991).

Growth has been the main thrust of policy, while redistribution and employment generation policies have been weak. Inequality was heightened in the oil boom era of the 1970s, and has been aggravated in the 1980s by a combination of collapse in oil income, austerity and adjustment-based measures. There has been a tendency for the rural–urban gap to be reduced, but this reflects more an overall deterioration in real incomes rather than improvements in rural living standard.

The first half of the 1960s, following independence in October 1960, saw relatively significant gains in GDP per capita with a growth rate of about 2.5 per cent per annum. The period 1960–70 did not witness on the whole substantial gains in per capita income because of the disruptions in production as a result of the Nigerian Civil War in the 1967–70 period. Per capita GDP increased at the rate of 0.6 per cent per annum from 1960–70. The Nigerian economy expanded fast during the 1970s, with GDP growing at an annual rate of 6.2 per cent (1970–77) and overall GDP per capita increasing at a rate of 3.6 per cent per annum in the 1970–77 period.

In this context, distribution of income has to take account of the contribution of different sectors to production. The drop in agricultural production from about 62 per cent in 1960 to about 25 per cent in 1975–76 was a product of an increase in the share of mining production from 1 per cent in 1960 to 32 per cent in 1975–76. Sectoral distribution of employment should follow an analysis of patterns of distribution of output. Agriculture absorbed 64 per cent of the total labour force in 1975. This marked a decline of the labour force in 1966–67 to about 70 per cent in 1970 and about 65 per cent in 1975. A fall in the labour force in agriculture usually accompanies growth of GNP per capita emanating from improvements in labour productivity in agriculture which may stimulate industrial production or occur as a result of pull factors arising from industrial investment and growth. In Nigeria the decline in share of the labour force in agriculture was due to differentials in income and public services between the rural and urban population. This gave rise to rapid rural–urban migration (Diejomaoh and Anusionwu, 1981, Chapter 3).

The increase in income inequalities as a result of the oil boom has been largely the result of the public expenditure pattern of the government which in the mid-1970s derived about 80 per cent of its revenue directly from oil production. The impact of production on the Nigerian economy was felt largely through the fiscal payments of the oil companies to the Nigerian government because the forward and backward linkages and direct employment effects of direct oil production were very limited in the economy (Diejomaoh and Anusionwu, 1981).

Reduction in income inequality in 1975–76 to 1978–79 was not very sharp.

In the 1980s inequality and poverty have been aggravated, following the collapse of oil export income and the imposition of austerity measures in 1982 and structural adjustment programmes (SAPs) and similar policies. There has been an increase in overall unemployment, a fall in real wages and minimum wages, intensifying urban and rural poverty. These changes have been more marked in the urban sector, which has faced a sharp slash in government expenditure. The rural–urban gap may have been reduced but this has taken place within the context of an overall fall in real income in the economy.

NOTE

1. Nigeria gained independence in 1960. The Nigerian Five Year Plans embrace the First Plan (1962–68), the Second Plan (1970–74), the Third Plan (1975–80), the Fourth Plan (1981–85) and the Fifth Plan (1985–90). The exchange value of the Naira, the Nigerian currency, has declined sharply since 1986 (following devaluation); thus, the Exchange Rate (Average) of the Naira to the $ was 0.894 in 1985, 4.016 in 1987, 8.012 in 1990, 9.5 in January 1992, 15 in 1992 and 19.5 in early October 1992.

8. Nigeria in the Postwar Period

Thinking on development in this period centres on the role of the state in organizing economic activity, and the influence of Keynesianism and neo-liberalism in shaping development goals. This is set within the context of the relationship between the global and the domestic economy.

THE GLOBAL–DOMESTIC RELATIONSHIP

Chapter 2 described the high hopes of Bretton Woods at the close of the Second World War, of creating a unique opportunity of reshaping the world economic system. Against this background, the interaction between the global and the domestic economy can be captured.

The impact of the global economy in bringing about change demands examining the extent to which favourable terms of trade, and increased inflows of resources, are used to induce changes in output, employment and poverty alleviation; and the ability to manage under unfavourable global conditions.

Nigeria's shift from exporting agricultural commodities, in the 'golden age', to minerals, from the early 1970s onwards produced profound changes in the terms of trade, creating scope for transformation from an agricultural to an industrial economy. There were significant surpluses in her balance of payments in the 1970s. Downward movements in terms of trade for Nigeria between 1980 and 1985 were held in check as a result of the fall in import prices. Indeed, the terms of trade improved in 1984. But lack of export dynamism in agriculture and manufactures and sharply increased domestic demand intensified the current account financing problems (Oshikoya, 1990, p. 74).

Nigeria's incorporation into the world economy can be traced to the pre-colonial period. This shaped the pattern of domestic specialization, trade and investment. The arrival of Portuguese traders in the seventeenth century and the beginning of the slave trade integrated Nigeria with the international system of exchange.

Colonial policies, which set out to maximize the extraction of surplus, moulded Nigeria's trading conditions, giving rise to a bias which persisted in the post-colonial period: exports of cash crops, a limited industrial structure and imports of manufactured goods and machinery.

Her economy at independence was marked by specialization in, and export of, 'base' products, and import of finished goods, comprising mainly manufactured consumer items and capital goods. The production of these base products had limited intersectoral linkages. In the early post-colonial era, between 1960 and 1965, the share of agricultural products in total exports was about 80 per cent (Ozo-Eson, 1988, p. 233).

The period from independence, in 1960, to 1973, as mentioned earlier, saw an emphasis on exports of agricultural products. In the 1960s Nigeria was a major exporter of cocoa, palm produce, groundnuts and cotton. Subsequently oil dominated exports, government revenues and development expenditure.

The rise of OPEC symbolizes the capacity of developing country commodity exporters to change radically their bargaining power. This aroused hope and enthusiasm, as expressed in Part 1, of redressing the unequal relationship between developing and developed countries. Indeed, between 1973 and 1981, OPEC took advantage of the world oil market to push the selling price of crude oil from below $5 per barrel to $40 per barrel (Federal Ministry of National Planning, 1983, p. 4).

Membership of OPEC enabled Nigeria to enjoy several advantages. Her experience of the oil industry was limited because of the absence of indigenous expertise. Unity among the large oil-producing countries was required to make the oil companies accept the participation agreement and control of production and pricing of crude oil. Nigeria was able to evolve her oil policy with ease because there was little pressure from transnationals.

During the 1970s, Nigeria was OPEC's sixth largest producer, contributing about 7 per cent of OPEC's total production (Wright, 1986, p. 19). Her fortunes from oil exports rose and fell in line with OPEC's rise and decline over 1973–88. She received increased prices for oil between 1971 and 1973. Over this period there was a rise of $3 per barrel in the price of oil, registering an increase of about 22 per cent. By April 1974, the price was about $11 per barrel and oil production had risen from less than 2 million barrels per day to 2.34 million barrels per day in mid-1974. Oil revenues almost quadrupled in nine months, the rise coming from higher prices, greater production and an increase in the government's share of the oil revenues from increased taxes, and royalties and ownership (Bienen, 1983, pp. 8–9). Exports (mainly comprised of oil) between 1970 and 1983 grew at an average rate of 30 per cent annually. Foreign exchange earnings from oil rose from $713 million in 1970 to $24.9 billion in 1980 (Wright, 1986, p. 19).

Oil conservation policies of the developed countries reduced the oil component of energy consumption. Such measures helped to reduce the world oil exports of the OPEC countries from about 31 million barrels per day in 1977 to about 17.5 million barrels per day in 1983, representing a drop in

OPEC's share of the market from 52 per cent to 33 per cent (Federal Ministry of National Planning, 1983, p. 4). Oil production from non-OPEC countries exceeded that from OPEC countries for the first time in 1981–82. World consumption of energy from oil fell from 51.4 per cent of total consumption in 1973 to 47.5 per cent in 1980. But that for nuclear energy increased from 1.3 per cent to 3.7 per cent, and for increased solid fuels from 20.7 per cent to 21.8 per cent (Federal Ministry of National Planning, 1983, p. 4). The rise of countries such as Mexico, as important oil producers, intensified this tendency.

Fluctuations in oil price from about $10 per barrel in 1986 to about $20 per barrel in 1988 caused considerable domestic disruption. OPEC has been struggling to control the output of its individual members to stabilize oil prices. OPEC's diminishing power, in comparison with the 1970s, illustrates that commodity power may be confined to a specific time span. Developing countries therefore have to maximize the advantage produced by booms in demand for their exports.

Oil export income in Nigeria fell sharply from Naira 13.63 billion in 1980 to Naira 5.83 billion in 1984, while the import bill over the same period increased from Naira 9.18 billion to Naira 11.52 billion (Oyaide, 1985, p. 3). The collapse in oil prices, as indicated earlier, heralded the debt crisis in Nigeria, with an external reserve position of $5.1 billion in 1979 being converted into an external debt of about $20 billion by 1983, when the country turned to the IMF for a $2.5 billion loan (Nyang'oro, 1986–87). Despite a deficit in the balance of payments, reserves enabled Nigeria to shelve the problem of how to finance imports.

Developments in the Middle East in 1991, with an embargo on supplies of oil from Iraq, led to oil prices rising to over $30 a barrel. This was temporary, as prices collapsed in the aftermath of peace in the later part of the year.

Domestic problems including ethnic conflicts, changes in government, wars and droughts may negate the effect of favourable global conditions. In contrast, positive domestic changes can reinforce external booms, or compensate for a deterioration in the world economy.

Competition between diverse ethnic and linguistic groups over state resources has far-reaching implications for inter-regional income distribution. Nigeria's federal–state structure has failed to accommodate the demands of such groups.

Blatant ethnic hostility has subsided but ethnicity remains an 'important filter through which the Nigerians perceive their political system and, furthermore, that the perception is normally blunt, stereotyped and unfavourable towards those of differing ethnic backgrounds' (Wright, 1986, p. 5). But care should be taken not to exaggerate the role of ethnic factors, as they are intrinsically related to economic conditions.

Changes in governments can destabilize the socioeconomic and political structure and disrupt the development process. Since independence in 1960 Nigeria's political system has been subjected to a number of changes (Bienen, 1983, p. 2).

Military coups, interspersed with periods of civilian rule, and a major civil war (1967–70), disrupted economic development. Civilian rule after independence in 1960 ended when the first military coup took place in January 1966. This was followed by another in July 1966. (An increase in oil revenues coincided with a period of reconstruction after the two military coups in 1966 and a bloody civil war fought between 1967 and 1970 (Bienen, 1983, p. 1).

The civil war led to an expansion of the armed forces which held power till the end of the war. The task of waging war, followed by reconstruction, sapped the government machinery. There was considerable war damage in the old Eastern region of Nigeria where many towns were badly damaged. However, Nigeria's small industrial base and its oil industry were not badly affected (Bienen, 1983, pp. 1, 9–10). Ethnic pressures gave rise to the creation of states.

The increases in the number of states from twelve to nineteen in 1976 strengthened the power of the federal government. Indeed, 'no longer did large regions confront and block each other as regional leaders jockeyed for national power.' Military leaders, in association with the civil service elite they chose, aimed to create a strong Nigeria in which the central government would formulate policy goals and implementation. Oil revenues furnished Nigeria's military and civil service leaders with the financial strength to carry out new plans (Bienen, 1983, p. 1).

A further military coup took place in July 1975. Elections were held over July–August 1979, ushering in an elected government, but civilian rule was abruptly ended in December 1983 by a military coup. This too was followed by a further military coup in August 1985. Military rulers have taken drastic economic and political steps to cope with Nigeria's severe external imbalance. These steps have conformed to stipulations laid down by international financial bodies and creditors.

THE STATE AND DEVELOPMENT

The state can play a significant role in organizing economic, social and political life. In a 'mixed' economy frame, both state and market forces are allowed full play. The virtues of the state versus the market in stimulating development have been fiercely debated, in particular the possibility of the state 'working with the market', in a complementary 'market-friendly' relationship.

A state can be 'neutral', or unbiased, if it does not act on behalf of a particular group or class. This is not realistic in developing countries where powerful urban- and rural-based classes, usually in alliance with factions of foreign interests, control the state.

In Nigeria colonial policies have played a significant role in moulding the state's character. A powerful trading-based middleman class was created, but a strong industrial class failed to emerge. Domestic and foreign bourgeoisie have used the state to further their own interests (Beckman, 1982). In the post-colonial era foreign capital in various forms, acting through middlemen, has continued to have a strong hold on the state. After the oil boom, bureaucrats reinforced their power, while foreign capital, too, primarily through multinationals, strengthened its hold.

Nigeria's incorporation into the global system through various phases, including colonialism, shaped and harnessed the forces of production. This has been to the advantage of foreign capital (Ojo, 1988, p. 123). The Nigerian bourgeoisie, which had the role of governing thrust upon it, has been basically a 'dependent, non-autonomous and derived class that does not own the means of production. It is also managerial rather than entrepreneurial in its activity' (Ojo, 1988, p. 123). The state has been dependent on multinationals to fill deficiencies in indigenous manpower.

The state in Nigeria should be seen as an arena and a system for 'peaceful, regulated intra-elite competition for money and opportunities for profit.' Moreover, the use of public office for private accumulation has been a key factor in the inability of African states to implement projects (Cooke, 1988). State bureaucrats in Nigeria, supported by both indigenous and foreign capital, have conformed closely to such forms of behaviour (Usman, 1983, p. 14). In this context, it is realistic to accept that a weak material base may have forced the bourgeoisie to adopt a dependent capitalist strategy of industrial development (Ojo, 1988, p. 126).

The belief that the state is all powerful in developing countries has been exaggerated. In Nigeria, the state has confined itself to specific regulative controls and to particular sectors, while allowing the private sector, including multinationals, to flourish. The call in the 1980s for curbing state intervention and giving full freedom to market forces simply represents an extension of an ongoing process. This has emerged in the aftermath of the collapse in Nigeria's oil exports, the sharp increase in external indebtedness and pressure from foreign creditors to execute structural adjustment programmes. Reductions in state expenditure, privatization, wage control and devaluation are essential preconditions of such policies (Roy, 1990a, pp. 45–7, 91–9).

In this context, the assertion by some leading economists that 'in good times as bad, Nigeria is administered excessively, inefficiently, corruptly, and ineffectively' is misplaced (Rimmer, 1985, p. 445). Discussion, therefore, over 'too much' state intervention is likely to confuse. The central question should, as noted in Part 1, focus on the quality of state action.

KEYNESIANISM AND NEO-LIBERALISM

State control over the economy in developing countries, as discussed in Part 1, has been closely linked to planned development. Emphasis has been placed on physical capital accumulation, drawing inspiration from Keynesian and Harrod–Domar models. The application of such concepts has been fraught with risk and uncertainty. Keynesian thinking was dominant over the first 30 years of the postwar period (1950–80). But from the 1980s onwards neo-liberalism, based on market forces, has provided the governing ideas for development.

Planning in Nigeria was built on Keynesian concepts. These have been obsessed with GDP, growth, capital–output ratios, foreign trade, creation of demand and 'similar mystifications of the Harrod–Domar and two gap models of Keynesian macroeconomics' (Onimode, 1979, p. 2).

Keynesian thinking on macroeconomic management in Nigeria has been embodied in the Harrod–Domar model, with its equation of development with rates of growth of income (GDP), its proportionality relation between growth of income and the rate of investment (or saving) and its use of the capital–output ratio to determine the proportion between capital formation and income growth (Onimode 1979, pp. 3–4; Fadahunsi, 1979: Introduction).

The assumptions of the Harrod–Domar model have not been related to factor endowments in Nigeria. Economists like Stolper, who have played a significant advisory role in Nigerian planning, accepted that the capital–output ratio which was popular in the country was too static for a dynamic planning problem, excessively aggregative, dubiously uncertain and inherently nebulous (Onimode, 1979, p. 7). 'Keynesian growthmanship' has ignored variables including the social relations of production, the development of productive forces, and sectoral and structural linkages (Onimode, 1988, pp. 211–12).

Planning in Nigeria could have benefited from Mahalanobis's (1955) model (based on investment and consumption goods) for India which was related to an earlier model by Feldman (1928) for the USSR (Fadahunsi, 1979, Introduction). The model and its origin are discussed more fully in the Indian case study (Chapters 12–16). The model stressed the capacity rather than the demand constraint on development, and the need to bias investment allocation consciously in favour of heavy capital goods industries. This could have facilitated the creation of a strong technological foundation (Onimode, 1979, p. 7). There was a statistical base to construct a four-sector model of the economy, which could have accommodated diverse projects. The model could have adapted Indian experience, including sectors for large-scale industrial production of investment goods; large-scale industrial production of consumption goods; the informal sector comprised of agriculture, small and household industries; and services including health, education, etc. (Fadahunsi, 1979, Introduction).

The emphasis on growth and capital accumulation was strongly influenced by planners such as Stolper who failed to grapple with redistributive goals. The five-year plans in the 1970s revealed awareness of the latter but it was seen primarily in regional terms, based on ethnic concerns.

The demise of Keynesian concepts and the rise of neo-liberal influences in the 1980s mirror a large-scale shift in thinking in economic policy. The new approach was embodied in the ideology of adjustment which proclaimed the virtues of market forces in governing the bulk of production and consumption decisions. Maximum exposure of the economy to global forces was called for. Nigeria already functioned within this frame. This thinking was rooted in neo-liberal thinking which provided the recipe for stabilization in case of balance of payments deficits and problems over meeting debt obligations. The policies call for contraction of economic activity, that is, a fall in the level of domestic output is assumed to reduce the demand for imported raw materials and investment goods, which by bringing about a decline in incomes is in turn expected to reduce demand for imports of consumer goods. In addition, curbs in government spending, increases in taxation, and reductions in the supply of credit to investing bodies and consumers are recommended (Hood, 1987, p. 335).

In the African context, where exports of most countries constitute a small proportion of total world supplies, higher domestic prices are meant to stimulate increased production. Africa's exports of minerals also demand lengthy investment programmes and most agricultural exports require several years before planting yield crops. One dimension of IMF's thinking has been that the balance of payments cannot be improved through devaluation alone, calling for accompanying policies to reduce money supply. This inevitably demands curbing public sector budgets (Hood, 1987, p. 335).

Devaluation and expenditure control are expected to correct the imbalance in international payments while maintaining full employment of resources. But short-term adjustment in African countries has depended heavily on reducing expenditure. This has adverse consequences for employment and incomes (Hood, 1987, p. 335).

Full-scale imposition of such economic theories has far-reaching economic, social and political consequences. Nigeria embraced such policies in the 1980s.

QUEST FOR SOCIAL JUSTICE

Growth has been the main motivation of policy makers in the postwar period. Despite attempts to strike a balance between growth and redistribution, the first has been dominant, with emphasis on the interregional rather than class dimensions.

Plans in Nigeria have echoed the need for combining redistribution with growth (Abba *et al.*, 1985, p. 141). Failure of adequate recognition of equity has been strongly voiced:

> A just and egalitarian society puts a premium on reducing inequalities in interpersonal incomes and promote balanced development among the various communities in the different geographical areas in the country. A distributive equity is, therefore, an important cornerstone in the set of national objectives for the government's programme of reconstruction and social reform. (Abba et al., 1985, p. 145)

It is naive to expect such proclamations to carry any conviction because of the dominance of regional conflicts. This is of enormous social and political significance and has served to divert attention from interpersonal inequality. Political analysts have accepted that

> interregional income differentials have been more important than inter-personal ones and that income differentials per se have been less contentious in Nigerian political life than disparities in endowments of schools, roads, health services, and the like (Bienen, 1983, p. 17)

The promise of better living standards or improvement in them (as by schooling) has been used as a political tool. Reduction of the differences in the levels of living have had a narrower appeal than condemnation of wealth derived from corruption, as in the general strike of 1964 and the period following the displacement of General Gowon in 1975. Equity has been perceived in terms of dispersing more opportunities and amenities evenly among the constituent parts of the federation (and of each state) rather than benefiting the poorer sections of the population. Sharing of public resources equitably among political units has also been easier than among occupational groups or income categories. Successful competitors have not been expected to be the classes who were already poor and disadvantaged (Rimmer, 1981, p. 67).

As explained in Part 1, growth has often failed to 'trickle down' to the majority of the population. The need to reconcile growth and redistribution continued to be voiced in Nigeria in the 1970s. This coincided with the state's acquisition of substantial oil revenues. Planners recognized this in the Third Plan (1975–80). Development was not simply growth in per capita income and it was possible to have a high growth rate in per capita income while the masses remained poor. The Fourth Plan (1981–85) also aimed to improve the living conditions of the Nigerian people, including a reduction in the level of unemployment and underemployment, more equal income distribution among individuals and socioeconomic groups and balanced development (Abba et al., 1985, pp. 145–6).

The Nigerian Constitution of 1978 placed responsibility on the state for meeting the basic needs of the population. Policies had to be devised to ensure that suitable and adequate shelter, food, a reasonable national minimum living wage and social security benefits were provided to all Nigerians (ILO, 1981, V, clause 16(2)).

This contrasts sharply with reality. Many historic (pre-colonial) Nigerian states were characterized by inequality, as was the colonial era and the years of independence before the oil boom. But the pattern of inequality has shifted from traditional mutual obligations and patron systems to greater individualistic wealth acquisition. This has been compounded by extensive corruption (Green and Singer, 1984, p. 288). The oil boom also created 'hideous displays of affluence' eroding moral and cultural values (Joseph, 1978, p. 238).

Basically, there has been no direct assault on inequitable distribution (Bienen, 1983, p. 8). Inequality and social justice have been discussed within the National Question, based on ethnicity and narrow parochial ideas (Bashir, 1988, p. 207).

DEVELOPMENT STRATEGIES

The thinking on development shaped the major strategies. A growth-based (capital accumulation) thrust has been dominant with limited emphasis on employment and redistribution. Although most of the goals have been laid down in development plans, they have been subject to considerable debate. The strategies have placed varying emphasis on the key industrial and agricultural sectors: import substitution and export-led growth. Programmes to increase employment, alleviate poverty and meet basic needs have been limited. Growth, which has been somewhat unstable, has been the main preoccupation; it was based primarily on exports, in the pre-1974 era on cash crops and subsequently on oil. Redistribution has been perceived primarily in interregional terms, mirroring the importance of inter-ethnic concerns. Foreign capital has been critical in moulding industrial and agricultural growth, reinforced by an inability to develop indigenous technology and management, while import substitution has been limited in changing the industrial structure.

9. Nigeria in the 'Golden Age'

THE GLOBAL CONTEXT

The golden age embodied a phase of dependence on trade based on exports of primary products. In the 1950s and 1960s the relevant indicator for Nigeria was the agricultural terms of trade. From 1960–69 the agricultural terms of trade showed a favourable upward trend but then declined by more than 50 per cent from 1968–72, indicating high and adverse external shocks. During this period, Nigeria recorded a trade surplus, which was helped by an increased export volume that compensated for the sharp decline in the terms of trade. The civil war over 1967–70 drastically reduced exports of palm kernels and palm oil. The sharp increase in earnings in Nigeria's agricultural exports, by 50 per cent from Naira 202 million in 1972 to Naira 303 million in 1973, mirrored the world commodity price boom and an increased volume of Nigerian exports (Oshikoya, 1990, pp. 74–5).

Agricultural exports were, till the mid-1960s, the main source of growth in the Nigerian economy. These contributed an average of 52.3 per cent to total GDP and 64.5 per cent to total exports. The average annual growth rate of real GDP was 6 per cent from 1960–67 and the growth of the agricultural sector was maintained from 1967–74. Nigeria had an average annual GDP growth rate of 5.5 per cent from 1967 to 1970 in spite of serious disruption of domestic production by the civil war (Oshikoya, 1990, pp. 75–6).

Nigeria's balance of payments was in deficit from 1960–65 (apart from 1962 when a surplus of Naira 58 million was recorded). The current account deficit averaged 5.2 per cent of GDP and 37.3 per cent of exports. External short-term and long-term borrowing played marginal roles in current account financing. Net foreign investment accounted for more than 80 per cent of total net capital inflows. The current account deficit rose from 7.3 per cent of GDP and 47 per cent of exports in 1966 to a surplus of 0.5 and 2.3 per cent, respectively, in 1973. The overall trade deficit of Naira 64 million in 1964 also became a surplus of 60 million in 1966. The trade surplus was maintained through 1972 and rose to Naira 1167 million in 1973. This was more than double the 1972 surplus of 478 million and more than triple that of 1971 (Oshikoya, 1990, pp. 69–72).

The country's total external debts rose from $US116.2 million in 1960 to $609.3 million in 1965; there was a slight decline to $602 million at the close of 1967. By 1970 total external debt fell to $567 million. Short-term debt as a percentage of total external debt was high in 1963: 28.1 per cent (Oshikoya, 1990, p. 87).

THE DOMESTIC ECONOMY

During the golden age growth was the central goal, with the main focus on agriculture and promotion of cash crop exports as the main source of government revenue. Attempts were made to stimulate specific industries, based on import substitution, and satisfy basic needs, like education and health. Over half of the resources in the First Plan were to come from foreign aid. But the results were disappointing, with military coups and a civil war damaging development.

Role of Agriculture

'Squeezing' agriculture as explained in Part 1 is a key mechanism for raising surplus. It has been instrumental in extracting savings for investment, and bringing about inegalitarian development.

The colonial state in Nigeria used the agricultural sector to siphon surplus, founded on cultivation of cash crops, including cotton, groundnuts and cocoa. A laissez-faire approach was adopted towards the food sector. Peasants were 'squeezed', with the bulk of the surplus being transferred to the metropolitan country.

Marketing boards facilitated the raising of surplus. These were established for cocoa (1947), cotton (1947), groundnuts (1947) and palm oil (1949), with the purpose of taxing agriculture. Over 1947–54, the Nigerian commodity boards accumulated surpluses of nearly £20 million, the bulk of which was kept in British securities. This was done at the expense of the peasantry, with 20–30 per cent and in some cases 60 per cent of potential producer prices being removed. The peasants also paid other taxes, fines and fees in the form of import duty on manufactured goods, poll and other taxes (Abdullahi, 1983, pp. 9–11).

Export volume quadrupled from 1945–55 and there was a sixfold increase in import capacity. The colonial state embarked on limited development planning, including production development boards for the investment of export trade surpluses. Some equity-based policies were implemented, based on welfare expenditure. Imports of manufactured goods was a conscious policy, but from the mid-1940s there was increasingly a shift towards import substitution. The industrial strategy was built around processing industries, such as oil mills, rice mills, and corn mills (Abdullahi, 1983, p. 8).

The mid-1950s saw the beginning of a phase of constitutional changes, with the emergence of strong regional and fiscal policies. The national commodity boards became regional commodity boards. Self-government was achieved in 1957 in the East and West and in the North in 1959. A transition from a colonial to a post-colonial economy was taking place. The indigenous bourgeoisie started taking over tariff, industrial and fiscal policies and allocation of foreign exchange. Agriculture continued to be 'squeezed'. It formed the basis of capital accumulation and was used for running the government and political parties, industrial and infrastructural development and conspicuous consumption (Abdullahi, 1983, p. 12). These developments need to be considered in relation to the use of public finance to support and subsidize the establishment of capitalist relations within Nigeria and merchant capital. The latter's resource base originated from past accumulation based on agriculture and shifted to manufacturing to protect its position in the Nigerian market (Abdullahi, 1983, p. 9).

PLANNING AND GROWTH

Post-colonial policies of the 1960s stemmed from attempts to transform the colonial economy. The First Development Plan (1962–68) of the Federation set out to produce a joint economic development plan programme (Ministry of Agriculture and Natural Resources Joint Planning Committee, 1974).

The plan emphasized growth, through conventional policies of raising savings and investment. This was to form the source for fulfilling redistributive ambitions. The aim was to surpass the past growth rate of the economy of 3.9 per cent per annum by targeting 4 per cent per annum or more. This was to be brought about by investing 15 per cent of the GDP. Per capita consumption was to be increased by about 1 per cent per annum. The emphasis was on accomplishing self-sustaining growth by the close of the Third or Fourth Plan. This was to be achieved by raising the domestic savings ratio from 9.5 per cent of GDP in 1960–61 to 15 per cent or higher by 1975. As explained in Part 1, this is a necessary step to bring about growth. Increased savings were to sustain the bulk of domestic investment and develop opportunities for domestic education, health and employment for all citizens and modernize the economy. The resources for the plan were to come from a combination of domestic and external sources (Ministry of Agricultural and Natural Resources Joint Planning Committee, 1974). Foreign aid was to compensate for inadequacies in domestic savings.

The central architect of the plan, W.F. Stolper, had a significant influence on emphasizing growth as the key thrust of the plan. Increasing per capita production was the 'supreme purpose of development planning' while 'questions of how to achieve it were not only logically distinct but also (which was more debatable) factually separate from questions of what to do with it.' Decisions on the use of resources had to fulfil the test of economic profitability. Employment, for example, could not be justified as providing occupation and earnings but only as a means of making net additions to output. Social aims could be fulfilled more fully by becoming productive (Rimmer, 1981, p. 42).

Limitations of an exclusive focus on capital formation, in the quest for growth, and the neglect of factors like health and nutrition, which could influence productivity, were discussed in Part 1. This was mirrored in the First Plan. It encouraged charging the public for the services provided. Those benefiting from a public service had to pay for it and productive investments were to be preferred to those whose links with production were indirect or weak. Free and subsidized services were not excluded but had to be confined to needs which were inherently non-economic. Education and health were key social sectors, where it was repugnant, and in some cases impossible to calculate precise economic returns. Indeed, 'human investment' arguments were not taken seriously; they did not lend themselves to quantification. Education and health care were seen as direct welfare benefits. The main force behind this was based on raising the productivity of the economy, in order to increase taxable capacity and hence the resources for investment (Rimmer, 1981, p. 42).

The First Plan gave scant attention to redistribution. The need for achieving 'a more equitable distribution of income both among people and among regions' was acknowledged. This recognition was qualified by highlighting the risk of premature preoccupation with equity, which could backfire and block development. Productiveness of the economy and autonomy of the nation were prominent but the distribution of welfare was neglected (Rimmer, 1981, pp. 43–4). Acceptance of a limit of 15 per cent in the investment rate was criticized by academics for being low. There was no call for development through structural change.

As explained earlier, the first half of the 1960s saw relatively significant gains in GDP per capita with a growth rate of 2.5 per cent per annum. But over the period 1960–70 per capita income increased at a rate of 0.6 per cent per annum because of the disruption in production arising from the Nigerian civil war in 1967–70. In this context, rural–urban inequality was prevalent in the 1960s, with a ratio of urban to rural per capita income of 2.5:1 in 1963, while the average income per head in rural areas during the 1960s was about

40 per cent of that of urban dwellers. The 1970s was to witness an aggravation of inequality between, and within, the sectors, fuelled by the oil boom.

Marginal attention was given to agriculture. Total federal and regional government expenditure on the sector was low. The type of growth desired was unclear and experts, who lacked adequate knowledge of the economy, held responsibility (Ministry of Agriculture and Natural Resources, 1974).

Political factors in Nigeria shaped the decision to pursue growth between 1950 and 1979. Policies were associated with graft. Men in authority, either directly or through the parties, benefited their supporters and home communities by using the provision of amenities, misappropriation of funds and nepotism in making appointments (Rimmer, 1981, p. 46). Public economic power and patronage were of great significance and became the mechanism for distributing benefits. Appointments to public office, especially in ministerial and public corporations, were of key importance (Rimmer, 1981, p. 48). Use of public office for private benefit was intensified after the oil boom.

10. Nigeria in the Era of 'Debt-led Growth'

The 1970s can be divided into the 'pre-oil' boom and the 'post-oil' boom periods. In both periods growth continued to be the main interest, forming the vehicle for increasing employment. Importance was attached to redistribution, particularly in the post-oil boom era. The urgency to satisfy basic needs remained weak, although education and health were not ignored. Import substitution in both the industrial and agricultural sector was intensified. Foreign capital and aid were prominent in both sectors, revealing underlying weaknesses in indigenous manpower and skills.

In practice, the strategies mirrored a sharp reduction in the role of agriculture in the economy, with exports of cash crops making way for oil. Import substitution in the industrial sector assumed importance but this was centred on minimizing dependence on consumer goods rather than capital goods. This phenomenon was described in Part 1.

Import substitution in the agricultural strategy, over the oil boom era, was aimed at reducing dependence on food imports, by using biological and mechanical technology.

THE GLOBAL CONTEXT

From 1974 onwards Nigeria's economic growth was fuelled by increasing oil exports, high public investment and massive external borrowings. Over 1974–78 the growth rate of real GDP averaged 6.5 per cent per annum; over 1970–82 the recorded average real GDP growth rate was 1.3 per cent. The oil price shock of 1973 improved Nigeria's terms of trade by more than 300 per cent and brought about a huge transfer of wealth to Nigeria. Agricultural export prices fluctuated considerably from 1977–80; oil prices increased by more than 168 per cent in the same period. Nigeria shifted in the early 1970s from an agricultural to an oil exporter: oil accounted for 97 per cent of exports. The contribution of oil to GDP increased from 2 per cent in 1960 to 31 per cent in 1980. After 1979 Nigeria experienced two successive increases in world oil prices: 64 per cent in 1980 and 13 per cent in 1981. But she also faced increases in international interest rates. The high and increasing oil prices were considered to be a permanent feature of international markets. In contrast, high international interest rates were considered to be temporary. This optimistic outlook prevailed till the third quarter of 1981 when oil prices started to weaken (Oshikoya, 1990, pp. 76–7).

Nigeria's balance of payments in the 1970s mirrors the impact of changes in her trading structure, with a shift from agricultural to oil exports. But this introduced considerable fluctuations in balance of payments, stemming from instability in income from oil. In this respect, there was confidence in a fall in oil income being only a temporary feature and being compensated in the future by a rise. Following the first big increase in the price of oil, there was a surplus of Naira 3012 million in 1974, in contrast to a surplus of only Naira 175 million in 1973 and a deficit of Naira 40 million in 1972. The subsequent years confirm the instability introduced by oil. Thus, by the close of 1975 the surplus dropped to Naira 158 million and there were deficits of 340 million and 447 million in 1976 and 1977 respectively. The deficit worsened in 1978, rising to Naira 1294 million. In contrast, a reversal in external transactions emerged in 1979 and 1980: with a surplus of Naira 1869 and 2402 million in the respective years (Oshikoya, 1990, pp. 72–3).

While oil-importing developing countries accumulated debts in the 1970s, Nigeria clearly gained significant income from the oil boom. She did not have to pursue 'debt-led' growth in this decade, but she too accumulated debts. There was considerable confidence in oil prices increasing.

Within this context, the early symptoms of Nigeria's debt problems started emerging in the 1970s.

First, external debts started mounting in the 1970s, although this fluctuated over the decade. There was a sharp increase in external debts in 1973, followed by a substantial decline in 1976, and an increase in 1977 (Table 10.1). From 1978 onwards total external debts showed a continuous upward trend.

Second, from 1970 onwards there was a rise in borrowing from private sources, while the share of concessional borrowing in total public debt declined. The grant component of total debt also fell sharply. Debt servicing, however, was not significant (Table 10.1).

These tendencies persisted into the 1980s, set against the decline in oil income from 1981 onwards. Access to oil revenues created the scope for transforming Nigeria into an industrial economy.

PLANNING AND DEVELOPMENT STRATEGIES: THE PRE-OIL BOOM ERA

Development goals of the state and the strategies for bringing them about were covered by the Second Plan (1970–74). Growth remained the main

Table 10.1 Total external debts outstanding ($US millions)

	1970	1971	1972	1973	1974	1975	1976	1977	1978	1979	1980	1981	1982	1983	1984	1985	1986
Total debts	567	651	732	1205	1274	1143	906	3146	5091	6235	8888	12039	12908	18586	18664	19522	24470
Concessional public debt (%)	64.6	62.9	58.7	35.9	36.9	43.6	57.5	55.9	21.7	15.2	11.7	7.1	4.5	3.6	3.5	3.3	2.8
Grant element (%)	21.5	40.3	26.1	24.0	41.7	13.3	8.2	10.7	−1.1	−3.6	−2.3	4.6	−0.3	−1.4	−0.3	3.0	6.2

Source: Extracted from Oshikoya (1990) Table 11, based on Central Bank of Nigeria, *Economic and Financial Review*, various issues.

focus, although the aims of establishing a more equitable society were not ignored. Inadequacies of growth and the need to incorporate redistribution were, as discussed in Part 1, major themes in global thinking on development in the 1970s.

Economic growth, as in the early 1960s, was the main interest of the Second Plan, but equity was not discarded. The motives behind the Second Plan can be understood more fully against the background of the civil war. Intensification of growth aimed to compensate for lost time and resources over the previous three years. The plan was geared towards achieving an annual growth rate set at a minimum of 6.6 per cent, with the industrial sector leading the way (Ojo, 1988, p. 130). Reconstruction of facilities damaged by war and promotion of economic and social development assumed great importance (Federal Republic of Nigeria, Third National Development Plan, p. 11).

The ideals of the plan were shared by many developing countries. These embraced the virtues of building a so-called strong and self-reliant nation and a democratic, just and egalitarian society. More concretely, the plan set out to accomplish a self-reliant strategy of industrialization. This demanded partial disengagement from the global economy and restructuring in three ways: use of deliberate policies which could change consumer values and consumption patterns, reducing inequalities in personal income distribution; and programmes to promote balanced development in the country (Ojo, 1988, p. 130). Asserting economic independence and defeating 'neo-colonial forces in Africa' were also emphasized. Progressively substituting Nigerian for foreign interests in the ownership and management of economic enterprises was of particular importance (Rimmer, 1981, p. 55).

The redistributive objectives of the Second Plan demand critical analysis. Despite the rhetoric of a 'just and egalitarian society', the focus was on economic growth and nationalism. Many compromises were made with foreign interests in this period (Bienen, 1983, p. 10). The core of the policy was to achieve the highest possible growth rate of per capita income. 'National autonomy' and 'social justice' were relegated to the background (Rimmer, 1981, pp. 54–5).

The aim was to move swiftly to the achievement of a minimum economic and social standard for every part of the country (Rimmer, 1981, p. 56). A tendency to ignore distributional concerns stemmed from the possible insignificance of the benefits which the poor could get from redistributing the income of the elite.

Employment creation, as explained in Part 1, was conceived not as an alternative to growth but as a proper instrument of growth. This thinking was envisaged not only to produce growth but also to help bring about equality in income distribution.

In Nigeria, however, full employment did not imply an obligation on the part of the government to secure wage employment for everyone. Rather, it was essential for all those who were of working age to be gainfully occupied according to the requirements of the economy and their skills (Rimmer, 1981, p. 56).

Nigerian planners succumbed to the traditional belief that in the long run growth would create jobs and eventually full employment. Employment-based programmes were deficient. The oil boom was accompanied by acceleration of migration to the towns. This was stimulated by relatively higher urban wages. Labour shortage in the rural areas was intensified, with adverse implications for increasing farm productivity.

Conflict between the objectives and hence the need to strike a balance was recognized, but 'a high overall rate of growth' remained, as in earlier plans, the main force. A fundamental conflict between growth and reduction of disparity was accepted (Rimmer, 1981, p. 54).

FOREIGN CAPITAL: PRE-OIL BOOM

In theory foreign capital may enable developing countries to gain access to resources, including finance, technology and management, and markets. As discussed in Part 1, the inflow of capital, in the form of aid and direct investment by multinationals, provided the main source of investment funds for developing countries. Whereas in the First UN Development Decade of the 1960s aid constituted 70 per cent of the total inflow, more than double the private inflow, the situation was subsequently virtually reversed. As mentioned in Part 1, typically 40–50 per cent of manufacturing industry in Latin America and Africa was controlled by foreign firms. The key concerns included the advisability of foreign investment in developing countries.

The experience of multinationals in Nigeria is common in many developing countries which face capital shortage or technological deficiency. They established themselves in import-substitution-based industries in Nigeria towards the close of colonial rule. Foreign capital here, in contrast to India, has had a significant influence on trade, manufacturing and agriculture, working through middlemen to reach bureaucrats and decision makers in control of policy. The transfer of resources out of the country by foreign capital, through legal and other means, has aroused deep emotions. In contrast to India too, lack of technological manpower in Nigeria has brought about dependence on multinationals.

The state adopted an 'open door' policy with a liberal outlook on imports, tariffs, investment and repatriation of profits (Kungwai, 1983). The oil boom exacerbated these tendencies. Inadequate indigenous managerial and administrative skill was a strong constraint on industrialization.

Policies to encourage 'a class of capitalists native to Nigeria' met many obstacles. These were initiated in the early 1970s, under the first Indigenization Decree in 1972 which prescribed complete or partial Nigerian ownership of business in a large number of activities. The inability of the state to plan effectively what it does not control, was recognized (Rimmer, 1981, p. 56). This intensified the attraction of substituting public Nigerian for foreign ownership.

Participation in the equity of private enterprises, or exclusive public ownership, was recommended as the mechanism for realizing such aims. Exploitation of 'strategic national resources' was to be under the exclusive control of the federal government alone or, provided it remained the dominant partner, in technical partnership with private concerns. Mining and manufacturing, although the exact nature of the latter was not specified, were the two sectors which the government wanted to control because of the need to shape the pattern of economic growth (Rimmer, 1981, p. 56).

In practice, Nigerian indigenization deviated from the norms laid down. The 1972 Decree gave indigenous business a protected position in commercial and low technology activities. But those who did not fall within this realm, or emerged after the oil boom, wanted a share of the proceeds rather than control. The latter was the goal of the state officials, both civil and military. Many businessmen were uncertain about the growth of the state sector. Individuals who could play a middleman role between the parastatals and foreign enterprises wanted the state to limit the extent of its control, so that they could acquire greater scope for their own equity participation (Bienen, 1983, p. 13).

In the 1970s the state welcomed collaboration with the private sector. Criticism of the latter was subdued. Socialization through nationalization was not encouraged.

The designers of the indigenization policies denied that the aim was to reduce private investment in the economy and initiate socialization. Rather, the military governments wanted to expand both the public and private sectors. Broadening the social base of capital ownership in the economy was on the agenda to enable Nigerians to share profits (Bienen, 1983). The government certainly wanted to dispel any notions about 'socialism' dominating Nigeria under the guise of the 'public' sector.

THE OIL BOOM AND 'DUTCH DISEASE'

Many developing countries, as explained in Part 1, confronted a period of debt-led growth in the 1970s. In contrast, Nigeria gained enormously from the power of OPEC, of which she was a member, to raise commodity prices. The increase in income from oil was a sudden boost. Such a phenomenon has given rise to the so-called 'Dutch Disease', a syndrome which can help to explain the Nigerian economy during the oil boom years and after the collapse of oil prices (Olopoenia, 1987, p. 43).

This theory suggests that rapid economic growth in one sector, such as oil, can attract a substantial shift of resources from sectors like agriculture. Historical patterns of development show that with economic growth will come a decline in the role of the agricultural sector in overall production and employment. But a sharp, temporary export boom can result in resource shifts which may be exaggerated and premature. The sector facing the boom draws foreign exchange into the economy, raising domestic demand and creating inflationary pressures on domestic prices. Relative prices of products in different sectors can be distorted by changes in the real effective exchange rate (Scherr, 1989, p. 544).

The real victim of the 'Dutch Disease' has been the formerly dynamic agricultural export sector and not the food sector. The latter was stable, although it was not capable of meeting the significant increase in domestic urban food demand (Scherr, 1989, p. 550).

PLANNING AND DEVELOPMENT DURING THE OIL BOOM

Nigeria gained from the unusually favourable terms of trade emanating from the sharp increase in oil prices. Clearly, this contrasts with oil-importing developing countries who faced adverse balance of payments and heavy external debts. Nigeria's experience should illustrate whether such 'golden opportunities' can initiate structural change. Access to increased revenues from oil exports enabled the state to expand its hold on the economy but at the same time the private sector, including foreign capital, was able to strengthen its links with the Nigerian state.

Emphasis on growth was retained in the 1970s. Despite concern for income distribution, inequality was heightened during this decade. This is discussed more fully in this section.

Following the oil boom, there was an increase in inflation in Nigeria. The exchange rate also appreciated. The foreign exchange rate is one of the most important macroeconomic policy instruments in balance of payments. Ni-

Table 10.2   Exchange rate indices (1973=100)

	Nominal	Real
1973	100	100
1974	106.8	101.1
1975	105.0	121.6
1976	104.3	141.0
1977	101.0	156.2
1978	101.6	177.2
1979	117.4	203.4
1980	120.8	202.2
1981	103.3	181.0
1982	98.2	191.6
1983	76.9	208.8
1984	81.4	263.7
1985	65.8	225.9
1986	19.8	73.9

Source: Based on Oshikoya (1990), Table 10.

geria adopted a fixed exchange rate policy effectively to adjust and correct balance of payments disequilibrium. The limited adjustments in the official nominal exchange rate coupled with the high inflation rate in Nigeria led to real exchange rates appreciating by more than 64 per cent between 1973 and 1984 (Table 10.2). The high real appreciation of the Nigerian currency led to imports being 44 per cent cheaper than non-traded goods in 1981 relative to 1972 and intensified the Dutch Disease phenomenon. By 1985 it became clear that the policy of stabilizing the nominal exchange rate through foreign reserve intervention was no longer feasible. The way in which the introduction of structural adjustment programmes (July 1986–June 1988) led to a large depreciation of the exchange rate from 1986 onwards is discussed later on.

Ambitions of bringing about not only an increase in income but also a more even income distribution, reducing unemployment, and securing a balanced, geographically dispersed development were reinforced by the Third Plan. Enthusiasm was expressed over diversification and indigenization of economic activity and an increase in the supply of high-level manpower (Federal Republic of Nigeria, *Third National Development Plan*, p. 29).

Access to substantial revenues from oil can explain the thirst for self-reliance. This was expected to achieve a rapid increase in the standard of living of the average Nigerian and place Nigeria in the list of developed countries of the world. Indigenization of economic activity was considered to be fundamental. There was increased emphasis on income distribution on a spatial and interpersonal basis (Ojo, 1988, p. 131).

Control of inflation following the oil boom also became an important policy concern in Nigeria. The 'Dutch Disease' syndrome, discussed earlier, intensified the problem of high inflation, which brought about an unprecedented rise in the general price level. Monetary expansion and disequilibrium of supply and demand of essential goods and constraints on domestic production were major contributory factors (Fashoyin, 1984, pp. 25–53). Import liberalization and exchange rate appreciation were adopted, both as a means of relieving the supply constraints and moderating the effect of imported inflation. Not until mid-1977 did the protection of the balance of payments position become a policy objective. This policy was abandoned by the early 1980s. The anti-inflationary measures were based on two assumptions. The first was that foreign exchange inflow from oil exports would continue undisturbed in the future; the second saw inflation in the Nigerian economy as being primarily of foreign origin (Olopoenia, 1987, p. 47).

The oil boom, as mentioned earlier, saw the beginning of Nigeria's overvalued exchange rate. Over the 1974–78 period, domestic prices were about 30 per cent higher than international prices; 1979–81 prices were 70 per cent higher and by 1982–83 prices were claimed to be more than double world prices (Scherr, 1989, p. 546). Devaluation of the currency became an important target for policy reform in the 1980s under the structural adjustment programme (1986–88).

Transformation of the economy was the main drive in the Third Plan (1975–80). This plan was launched against a background of buoyant financial resources, following sharp increases in the price of crude oil and Nigeria's level of production. On the eve of the Third Plan in March 1975, the country's oil production was at a record level of 2.3 million barrels per day while the price per barrel stood at $14.69, having risen from $3.56 in 1973. Production was projected to grow at a modest rate to reach 3.0 million barrels per day by the close of the plan period (Federal Republic of Nigeria, *Fourth National Development Plan:1981–85*, p. 3). This formed the basis of tenfold increases in planned capital expenditure, from Naira 3 billion in the Second Plan to Naira 30 billion in the Third Plan; it was a mere Naira 2.2 billion in the First Plan (Federal Ministry of National Planning, 1983, Chapter 1:1; Federal Republic of Nigeria, 1981–85, p. 3). The share of the public sector in the Third Plan was initially set at Naira 20 billion (Federal Republic of Nigeria, *Fourth National Development Plan*, p. 3). The importance of foreign aid and private foreign investment was assumed to be insignificant (Ojo, 1988, p. 132).

Optimism generated by oil revenues gave impetus to the development of the productive capacity of the economy and raising living standards. Emphasis was placed on building economic and social infrastructure required for self-sustaining growth in the long run when resources might become scarce (Federal Republic of Nigeria, *Third National Development Plan*, pp. 30–31).

The sensitivity of an open economy to changing export prices is mirrored in Nigeria's experience. Fluctuations in oil prices reduced planned targets. Demand for oil plummeted with adverse consequences for prices. Oil producers had to cut back output. Nigeria's production dropped sharply by 35 per cent to 1.5 million barrels per day barely five months after the Third Plan was launched. The price of crude oil fell by as much as 12 per cent. The impact of this was an absolute decline of about Naira 1819.6 million in the contribution of the oil sector to GDP in the fiscal year 1975–76. There was some improvement between 1976 and 1977, but another round of decline surfaced in 1978 when production fell because of a fall in demand. These changes in the levels of production distorted the flow of financial resources, making it necessary to borrow from the Euro-dollar market and multilateral institutions such as the World Bank (Federal Republic of Nigeria, *Fourth National Development Plan*, p. 3).

Political changes can create instability in development policies. Barely four months after the Third Plan was launched, there was a change in Nigeria's government. This led to a pause in executing the plan which was just beginning to take off. Plan implementation was actually halted in some states to facilitate stocktaking, while at the federal level the new administration ordered a plan review as early as October 1975. During the review implementation was almost halted (Federal Republic of Nigeria, *Fourth National Development Plan*, p. 4).

Actual investment patterns bore little relationship to the avowed intention of reducing personal income inequalities or promoting balanced development. Planning mirrored the economic, social and political preferences of the national elite (Ojo, 1988, p. 133).

Despite heavy expenditure, the sectoral balance did not bring about structural change founded on industrialization.

Role of Industry

Import substitution has certainly been a chief means of industrializing developing countries. Access to resources is an essential precondition for realizing plans for transforming the pattern of industrial growth. This usually demands substituting the production of capital for consumer goods.

This pattern can be detected in Nigeria. A policy of domestic production of consumer goods was adopted. Capital goods were imported for this purpose. Lack of access to indigenous technology, manpower and skills led to dependence on multinationals which controlled key industries.

Nigerian manufacturing, however, has been biased against heavy and basic industries. This feature has intensified her technological dependence (Ekuerhare, 1984). The state encouraged high tariffs on consumer goods imports relative to capital and intermediate goods. The latter were imported to produce consumer goods and have led to the type of strategic dependence noted in many studies on Latin America. Imports of manufactured items were replaced by imports of equipment, raw materials and spare parts, without which Nigeria's manufacturing would be halted (Abba et al., 1985, p. 53). This experience has been shared, as noted in Part 1, by many developing countries.

Composition of output reveals a bias towards low value-added manufacturing and assembly types of industries. Non-durable consumer goods industries such as food, beverages, tobacco, beer, spirits and textiles dominated the manufacturing structure. These industries were responsible for 51.5 per cent, 44 per cent and 43.1 per cent of manufacturing value added in 1964, 1975 and 1978. This contrasted with industries which made insignificant contribution to value added, including machinery and transport, metal fabrication, chemicals, petroleum, energy and engineering industries (Ekuerhare, 1983; 1984; 1980, pp. 6–8). Critical investments in projects such as iron and steel, petrochemicals and machine tools were either executed poorly or not at all. Inability to implement planned development of the industrial sector was a significant obstacle to activating backward and forward linkages in the economy. Alternative manufacturing strategies to create industrial self-sufficiency were not devised. The production of basic materials required by the majority, including food, clothing and drugs, intermediate inputs for industry, agricultural tools and machines for the production of other machines should have been given higher priority (Abba et al., 1985, p. 65).

Multinationals, acting through their subsidiaries or through local joint venture partners, have been dominant in the big industrial, trading and agricultural sectors. For instance, in 1976 they owned 39.2 per cent of the oil, 57 per cent of the manufacturing, 72 per cent of the trading, and 70 per cent of the agricultural sectors. Foreign investment in 1977 in oil, manufacturing and trading formed 25.4 per cent, 25 per cent, and 29 per cent of the total investments in the respective sectors (Kungwai, 1983, p. 17). Dependence on multinationals was reinforced by the inability of the state to bring about planned outputs in specific projects, including proper execution in iron and steel industries (Abba et al., 1985, p. 67).

The scope for establishing an integrated relationship between the industrial and agricultural sectors is a subject of considerable interest. The interaction between the two sectors is closely linked to resource-based industrialization. This has been examined in Nigeria with particular reference to the long-term implications for reducing imports of manufactured and industrial goods and dependence on foreign manpower based on a study of the textile and cotton industry (Andrae and Beckman, 1987; Fadahunsi, 1986; Roy, 1990c).

Doubts have been expressed about the shift in agricultural policies towards large investments which have either completely bypassed the peasantry, or restructured and subordinated peasant land and labour through contractual arrangements and regulations governing land control. Central to such policies is the removal of controls over direct foreign investments in this sector and exploitation by authorities, on behalf of new domestic and commercial investors, of ambiguities in existing land legislation (Andrae and Beckman, 1987). Proposals to generate resource-based industrialization have centred on elimination of foreign products and production processes which are unnecessary for Nigeria. The list includes various traditional and modern (foreign) consumption and production goods and services in agriculture, manufacturing, building and construction, transport, education and health. Agrobased industries, including food, textiles, paper and rubber, are of critical importance. Simultaneous development of agriculture and agro-based industry could provide sufficient funds for building heavy industry (Fadahunsi, 1986).

Role of Agriculture

In contrast to India, immediately after independence, Nigeria pursued a laissez-faire approach towards the food sector (Roy, 1990a, pp. 52–3). But increasingly she was unable over the 1970s to meet domestic food requirements and was forced to depend on imports. In this context, import substitution emerged in the agricultural sector. As explained in Part 1, modern technology can boost food production and Nigeria used this strategy, from the early 1970s onwards, to meet demand for food. This thrust was intensified from the mid-1970s onwards, following access to oil revenues. After 1980, the two key technology-based strategies were the River Basin Development Project, based on large-scale irrigation, and the Agricultural Development Project. But success has been limited in achieving self-sufficiency compared with India because of defects in shaping and executing policies. Nigeria's experience highlights the case of many countries which have adopted intensive farming founded on imported inputs. Access to oil revenues enabled her to finance such farming but problems emerged after the collapse, from the early 1980s onwards, of oil export income (Roy, 1990a, pp 60–68; 74–9).

The oil boom sharply accelerated the technological drive in agriculture, against a background of stagnation of traditional cash crop exports. The 'green revolution' (April 1980) symbolized the drive to increase food production through modern technology. The output, self-sufficiency and equity implications of such strategies have been critically questioned (Roy, 1990a).

Nigeria confronted falling food production, as shown earlier, with either stagnation or slow growth in aggregate food crop production over 1970–82; the rate of growth was considered to be less than any plausible population growth rate (World Bank, 1985, p. 13). The traditional agricultural exports collapsed. Following the oil boom, the agricultural growth rate was near zero until 1980 (Singh, 1983).

Imports of cereals rose sharply. The annual average level of imports between 1977 and 1979 was over three times that between 1974 and 1976 (Sender and Smith, 1984, pp. 8, 34). By 1980, imports of wheat, maize and rice constituted the principal grains, accounting for 33 per cent of all grains supplied in the country (Kwanishie, 1983, pp. 18–19). In terms of total food requirements, which included not only grains but also root crops and staples, imports accounted in 1982 for a share of 11 per cent: wheat being 7 per cent and rice and maize 4 per cent (World Bank, 1985, p. 23).

The Agricultural Development Project was an aid package, based on collaboration between the federal and state governments and the World Bank; the latter had an important role in the conceptualization of the model. The project divided potential beneficiaries into three distinct groups: the 'progressive' (less than 100 acres), the 'large-scale' (more than 100 acres) and the 'traditional' groups; the first two were expected to be the main participants, in terms of taking advantage of the project. The large-scale beneficiaries included many who had urban-based political, bureaucratic and business links. They were able to reinforce their power (Roy, 1990a, pp. 147–52; Beckman, 1987, pp. 118, 132).

The River Basin Development Project embodied large-scale irrigation, using biological and mechanical inputs coupled with infrastructural ones: the latter included large dams for irrigation, land-clearing equipment, etc. The project aimed to replace imported cereals through dry-season farming. A number of such irrigation projects were started in the mid-1970s and were subsequently spread throughout the country (Roy, 1990a, pp. 67–8;140–42).

The project was managed by the state but relied on imported large-scale capital and expatriate skills to run it at the village level. The design and construction of the project were often left to multinational agro-based firms (Beckman, 1987). The impact on output, imports and equity has been highly controversial, with a subsequent pruning of the project.

EMPLOYMENT AND POVERTY STRATEGIES

Part 1 described the direct assault in the 1970s on poverty: employment and basic needs programmes. Nigeria could have given serious attention to such approaches but there were no large-scale programmes. Resources allocated to basic needs such as education and health faced many constraints. There was no attempt to embrace 'basic needs' till the close of the 1970s (Roy, 1987, pp. 13–16).

Inequality was heightened, as shown earlier, during the 1970s. The explosive growth of oil resulted in the rural population's average income per head in the mid-1970s being only about 10 per cent of urban average income. Oil production had limited forward and backward linkages and direct employment effects were very limited. Although the mining sector made a significant contribution to total output, its share in total gainful employment was only 0.4 per cent in 1975, while manufacturing and distribution absorbed 16.8 per cent and 12.2 per cent respectively (Diejomaoh and Anusionwu, 1981, Chapter 3).

Income inequality increased between 1970 and the mid-1970s. The Gini coefficient was estimated to have increased from the 1970 level of 0.55 to about 0.7 in 1975/76. The magnitude of interpersonal income inequality in the rural population was low with Gini coefficients of probably around 0.3 because of widespread impoverishment throughout the population. Village studies have revealed increasing inequality between and within cash and food crop farmers. Export crop farmers, producing primarily cash crops, have had a mean household income which was five times above that of food farmers. Recent studies, however, show that there are no significant differences in mean income (Collier, 1988, pp. 196–7, 206). Development of commercial agriculture in grain-producing regions of northern Nigeria reveal that the introduction of World Bank-sponsored agricultural development projects to boost maize production have sharpened inequality between small and large farmers (Roy, 1990a: 147–52, 157–66).

Social programmes have not been given priority, with no direct action to reduce poverty. Over 1974–79, the number of urban households below the poverty line increased sharply, perhaps by as much as 100 per cent, implying an increase in the proportion in absolute poverty nationally (Green and Singer, 1984, pp. 119, 289). Provision of basic needs such as education and health has increased, but has failed to make a breakthrough in alleviating poverty. The weaknesses of such programmes have been pointed out by the ILO (ILO, 1981) and by researchers on Nigeria (Fadahunsi, Olowononi and Roy, 1985).

Some employment-oriented projects were articulated in the Third Plan. Construction projects, which were expected to absorb a large amount of labour, formed the bulk of the plan (Federal Republic of Nigeria, *Third National Development Plan*, p. 31). The plan strategy specified that the public sector was to provide subsidized facilities for the poorer sections of the population. These programmes were geared towards raising the living standards of the poor and constituted a more practical step towards redistributing income compared with other measures. Fiscal policies including progressive taxation were also adopted. Universal free education was also on the agenda in the plan.

Equity in Nigeria, in practice, has meant dispersing more opportunities and amenities equally among the constituent parts of the federation (and of each state) rather than benefiting poorer sections of the population (Rimmer, 1981, p. 67).

Oil revenue distribution and employment generation have been concentrated in the urban areas among a growing middle class (Scherr, 1989, p. 553). In the rural sector, especially in the poorer states, services have been very limited, except for primary education. Rural investment since independence has been focused on settlement schemes, plantations and similar large-scale, modern approaches. These have excluded poor rural households (Green and Singer, 1984, p. 289).

In the urban sector, expansion of services has not been able to keep pace with urban growth. Low investment allocations have tended to be underspent. The quality of both public (e.g. water and sewage) and private (e.g. low-income area housing) infrastructure has declined. The fall in average food availability and the rise in absolute poverty indicate a deterioration (Green and Singer, 1984, p. 289).

Nigeria has been plagued by problems of poor nutrition, health care delivery, housing and education. Access to good nutrition, health, housing and education has been governed by market power. This theme has worked against the poor. Basic needs have also been divorced from basic rights. The fundamental factor is the control exercised by different groups over the socioeconomic system (Fadahunsi, Olowononi and Roy, 1985; Roy, 1987, pp. 13–16).

Concern over basic needs took a new turn when, towards the close of the 1970s, the National Planning Office in Nigeria commissioned a study by the ILO on 'Basic Needs in Nigeria' as a background to the Fourth National Development Plan: 1981–85 (Fadahunsi, Olowononi and Roy, 1985, Introduction; ILO, 1981).

Basic needs measures were unable to reduce inequality. Nigeria was able to avoid 'debt-led growth', but the decade was certainly one of 'lost opportunity'.

11. Nigeria in the 'Lost Decade'

The 1980s were described in Part 1 as being a 'lost decade' and a movement away from development, in terms of growth, employment, redistribution and poverty reduction. These were replaced by programmes primarily to reduce external debts, based on adjustment programmes.

Compared with many developing countries, Nigeria benefited in the 1970s from favourable terms of trade, because of the oil boom. This created room for socioeconomic transformation. The collapse of oil revenues in the early 1980s exposed the deep-seated structural weaknesses, including a backward agricultural sector, an inadequate capital goods industry, a lack of indigenous skills and technology and dependence on a single commodity for exports. Extensive poverty prevailed in the country.

THE GLOBAL CONTEXT

Oil continued in the 1980s to be the main export and provider of government revenue. The collapse in oil prices exposed the vulnerability of the economy.

Optimism prevailed, till the third quarter of 1981, of oil prices remaining high. From this year onwards oil prices declined sharply. The world oil market remained depressed till 1983 when a large percentage of the country's external debts were due. Oil prices started to slide downwards. The terms of trade fell between 1980 and 1985 but were held in check by a fall in import prices. In fact, the terms of trade improved in 1984. There was a lack of export dynamism in agriculture and manufacturing and sharply increased domestic demand aggravated Nigeria's current account financing problems (Oshikoya, 1990, p. 77).

Oil revenues as a percentage of total revenue increased from a mere 4 per cent in 1961 through 60 per cent in 1973 to 82 per cent in 1980. Government expenditure, in relation to GDP, increased from a low of 6.3 per cent in 1963 to 30 per cent in 1980, falling to 26.2 in 1982. Government spending through development plans increased domestic absorption sharply and also resulted in external disequilibrium.

Severe balance of payments problems faced Nigeria from 1981 onwards. The current account surplus in 1980 turned into a deficit of Naira 3708 million in 1981, increasing to Naira 4880 million in 1982. As a proportion of GDP, a current account surplus of 5 per cent in 1980 became a deficit of 10 per cent in 1982. External reserves at the close of 1983 were hardly enough to meet one month's import bill. Nigerian importers found it difficult to secure credit from overseas creditors.

Total external debts as a proportion of GNP increased steadily from 9 per cent in 1980 to 21 per cent in 1983. The ratio fell slightly in 1984 but between 1985 and 1986 more than doubled. This mirrored the impact of the oil shocks. Nigeria's ratio of international reserves to total external debt stood at 120 per cent in 1980 declining to 5.5 per cent in 1986. The ratio of total public external debt to exports of goods and services increased from 15.3 per cent to almost 300 per cent in the same period. Nigeria's long-term public debt service ratio increased from 1.8 per cent in 1980 to 31 per cent in 1985. It then fell to 18 per cent in 1986; this decline resulted mainly from deliberate efforts by the Nigerian government to put an official ceiling on the debt service and reflected an increasing recourse to debt rescheduling (Oshikoya, 1990, p. 89).

PLANNING AND DEVELOPMENT

The collapse of income from oil exports led to abandoning ambitious development plans. In contrast to the past, oil prices failed to recover to their former high levels and the state was confronted with massive external debts. There was a marked shift in priorities and strategies. The domestic economy was coerced, through deflationary policies, into re-establishing equilibrium in Nigeria's external balance, within the context of an economy driven by market forces, while the state's role was curbed.

A rapid increase in the nation's productive capacity and improvement of the standard of living of the people was a main theme of the Fourth Plan (1981–85). The weaknesses of the previous plans were acknowledged (Federal Republic of Nigeria, *Fourth National Development Plan*, p. 3).

The plan was very ambitious. It set out to reorganize the economy, accommodating growth and distribution, including providing a number of basic needs. This rested on a planned capital expenditure of Naira 82.5 billion which was well above that of the previous plan. Emphasis was placed on increasing real income, establishing a more even distribution of income, reducing unemployment, reducing dependence on a narrow range of activities and greater self-reliance. Agricultural production and processing were to continue receiving 'the highest priority', to feed people without massive imports and supply raw materials to agro-based industries (Federal Republic of Nigeria, *Fourth National Development Plan*, pp. 37–9). Human capital, and particularly education and manpower development, was to be the next priority, given the shortage of skilled manpower.

Manufacturing was to get 'appropriate emphasis', with the aim of diversifying the national economy. Implementation of large-scale industrial projects, such as steel and petrochemicals, was to be vigorously pursued, with greater encouragement to the private sector to invest more in manufacturing. A move away from overdependence on the petroleum sector was also planned, including developing exports such as textiles as well as the traditional ones like cocoa.

The collapse of oil export income can be highlighted by the sharp contrast between targets and actual achievements of the Fifth Plan, particularly in manufacturing, agriculture, construction and transportation. Some recorded negative growth (Table 11.1).

Table 11.1   Fourth National Development Plan (1981–85): targets and actual growth rates

	Plan target	Actual (p.a.)
Agriculture	4	1.2
Mining and quarrying	2	8.5
Manufacturing	15	2.5
Utilities	15	−8.0
Construction	5	−15.4
Transportation	12	−12.0
Communications	15	−5.5
Commerce	10	−5.5
Housing	8	−9.3
Services	2	4.3
GDP (at factor cost)	7.2	2.9

Source: Okigbo (1989). Based on Federal Ministry of National Planning Data.

The laudable aims of the plan were shattered, exposing the sensitivity of an open economy to changes in global demand. This was exacerbated by domestic problems. First, 86 per cent of capital formation was to be undertaken by various levels of government, with the federal government undertaking only 50 per cent. But local governments were poorly structured, staffed and ill-equipped to supervise, monitor and implement federal or state projects. Second, most capital projects had not been studied in detail and investment plans were not clear. Third, a number of aberrations and reverses which characterized Nigeria's Second Civilian Republic also vitiated the plan. Mismanagement and fraud were critical problems. By the end of 1983 Nigeria's debts reached $17 billion. Nigeria contemplated for the first time in over a decade seeking loans and foreign aid. The near collapse of the economy led to the civilian administration (1979–83) under President Shegu Shagari being deposed by a military coup in December 1983 (Ojo, 1988, pp. 138–40).

The emergence of the crisis which confronted the Nigerian economy in the early 1980s mirrored the symptoms of deeper problems. These came to the surface with the collapse of oil prices in 1981. The Odama Report in 1983 highlighted some of the major global and domestic causes of the crisis (Federal Ministry of National Planning, 1983).

Nigeria's ability to become self-reliant was blocked by her economic and sociopolitical structure. Fundamental structural changes were required. A critical factor was the decline of revenue from oil exports and the very high level of outflow of external resources due to rapid expansion of imports from 1980 onwards. The decline of OPEC's share in the world oil market from 52 per cent in 1977 to 33 per cent in 1981–82 underpinned the collapse of Nigeria's export income. A combination of factors led to the outflow of reserves from 1980. These included imports of goods and services, repatriation of profits, evasion, uncoordinated and disorganized policy of import licensing and foreign exchange disbursement and foreign loans. The high level of payments for wages, salaries and allowances, and benefits unrelated to increases in productivity, were contributory factors. Furthermore, inflated contracts and projects which cost 300 per cent more than those in East and North Africa and about 400 per cent more than those in Asia posed critical problems. The low internal generation of revenue hampered the economy and the poor performance of the manufacturing and agricultural sectors inhibited development. In spite of recognizing the problems facing Nigeria, the Odama Report called for rolling back the state (Federal Ministry of National Planning, 1983). The role of multinationals in controlling industries was ignored. Moreover, the reasons for the wastage of oil resources were not confronted: smuggling, hoarding, evading taxation, benefiting from imports of assembly plants, inflated contracts and general government policy. The Nigerian private investor plus his foreign partners, as well as private investors holding high public office, have been held responsible for having brought about a collapse of the government's finances. Those ruling Nigeria in the period 1973–83 had been shifting their wealth to Western Europe and North America (Usman, 1983).

ADJUSTMENT STRATEGIES

The role of adjustment in Nigeria can be understood more fully by putting it in the context of similar programmes in Africa. The IMF and the World Bank have been the main initiators of this policy. From 1979 onwards the IMF started devoting a significant percentage of its financial facilities to sub-Saharan Africa, including conditional loans. It established the structural adjustment facility (SAF) in March 1986, effective from December 1987 onwards. This facility set out to provide credit to low-income countries with protracted balance of payments problems. The main impetus was on assisting eligible member countries to undertake strong three-year macroeconomic and structural adjustment programmes to improve their balance of payments position and foster growth (Moyo and Amin, 1989, p. 244).

As discussed in Part 1, the virtues of structural adjustment programmes (SAPs) are highly controversial. Both the IMF and the World Bank, but particularly the former, placed excessive weight on repayment of external debts. It is essential to define 'adjustment' more closely: it can be looked at simply in terms of repayment of debts or perhaps wider concepts of 'development' need to be included (Roy, 1990d, p. 4). The Economic Commission for Africa (ECA) and others have critically questioned World Bank findings which suggest that there has been a better overall economic performance in countries that pursue strong reform programmes than in those that do not. The ECA concluded that GDP in countries with so-called strong structural adjustment programmes recorded an overall negative average annual growth rate (about 1.5 per cent) during the period 1980–87 (United Nations Economic Commission for Africa, n.d, pp. 22–3). Moreover, reductions in state expenditure are exemplified by the experience of African economies including Kenya, Malawi, Zambia and Ghana. While expenditure on defence, public order and general administration shows an increase in capital spending between 1980 and 1981 and 1986 and 1987, housing, health and agricultural services have been cut more than the average over the same period (Mosley and Smith, 1989, p. 334).

African countries which adopted 'structural adjustment' policies have confronted resistance from workers, who have opposed wage freeze, privatization, public sector cuts and increases in the prices of essential commodities and services (Bangura and Beckman, 1989, p. 1).

In Nigeria the programme emerged against a background of domestic political chaos and austerity measures to stabilize the economy. The SAP represents a departure from the norms laid down in the Fourth Plan and an attempt to revive traditional agricultural exports. Reducing state control and resorting to market forces have assumed dominance. The programme has moulded Nigeria's future development.

The SAP in Nigeria (July 1986–June 1988) was shaped against a background of the failure of policies to resuscitate the economy from April 1982 onwards. The Economic Stabilization Act of April 1982 (amended in January 1983), under the civilian government of Shegu Shagari, was followed by various fiscal and monetary policies under military regimes: first under Buhari, who assumed power in a coup in December 1983, and second under Babangida, who overthrew Buhari in August 1985.

The Economic Stabilization Measures (April 1982) included wide-ranging fiscal, monetary and other measures to overcome the severe financial pressures facing Nigeria. In anticipation of an IMF $2.5 billion programme, the Nigerian authorities implemented an austerity and recovery programme in 1983 (Nyang'oro, 1986–87).

Buhari's policies rested on orthodox deflationary measures. These were based on reducing government expenditure through massive retrenchment of public service employees to cut the wage bill, withdrawal of state subsidies on health and education, coupled with reintroduction of school and hospital fees, and a unilateral wage freeze. Meticulous collection of taxes was put into effect. Emphasis was placed on repayment of short- and long-term loans, and in particular trade backlogs. A campaign under the banner of 'war against indiscipline' underpinned the policies. These policies were pursued within the context of continuing negotiations with the IMF (Olukoshi and Abdulraheem, 1985, pp. 96–7).

Buhari's policy of imposing strict foreign exchange regulations, as an alternative to IMF conditionalities and dependency, was unpopular. It was backed by moral persuasion and discipline. The measures, which were harsh, were reinforced in 1984. They failed to arrest the economic decline.

Babangida pursued many policies similar to those of his predecessor. However, he tackled the question of whether to take the IMF loan or not with greater sensitivity, by asking people to vote on it. The answer was a decisive 'no'. In practice, Babangida executed policies which met many of the basic 'conditionalities' laid down by the IMF. Arrangements were made for IMF 'enhanced surveillance' without (for domestic political factors) the drawing down of the IMF loan. Debt rescheduling operations covered the period to the end of 1987, and were followed by negotiations to reschedule maturities due in 1988–90 (Economist Intelligence Unit 1989, p. 13).

The SAP in Nigeria embodied the basic ingredients of the IMF/World Bank adjustment package including strengthening demand management, stimulating domestic production, broadening the supply base, and pursuing a realistic exchange rate policy.

The core policies embodied (a) correcting the serious overvaluation of the Naira through the setting up of a viable and substantial second-tier foreign exchange market (through which the exchange rate would broadly be set by market forces in auctions held by the Central Bank of Nigeria) coupled with adjustment of the official rate; (b) convergence of the various official exchange rates as soon as possible; (c) overcoming public sector inefficiency through improved public expenditure control programmes and speedy rationalization of the parastatals; and (d) relieving the debt burden and attracting foreign capital while keeping a lid on foreign loans (Federal Government of Nigeria, n.d., pp. 9–10). The SAP was not just an economic phenomenon but posed critical socioeconomic and political questions. In Nigeria's case, the considerable overvaluation of the Naira since the oil boom years in the 1970s could justify devaluation. Such policies may be negated by other factors. A study of some African countries suggests that devaluation may add enough to the inflation rate to negate itself in less than a year (Godfrey, 1985, pp. 36–7). Devaluation is also unlikely to lead on its own to a sizeable increase in exports without fundamental changes in domestic production capacity.

Other SAP conditions included massive retrenchment, trade liberalization, subsidy withdrawal, privatization of public enterprises, merging of second-tier foreign exchange markets (SFEMs), two rates of exchange into one rate, i.e. about N4 = $1.00 and the freeing of interest rates, both in July 1987. As mentioned earlier, Nigeria has continued to confront debts and debt-servicing problems.

Introduction of SFEMs was followed by export licensing abolition. The devaluation increased import expenses and led to a rise in production costs. There was an escalation of costs which was passed on to consumers. Major tariff cuts at the same time as SFEMs aimed to stimulate efficiency. Well-protected industries were exposed to increased competition from imports. Many small- to medium-sized companies were hit by SAPs (Economist Intelligence Unit, 1989).

The initial indicator of the economy's response to structural adjustment may be promising but it conceals massive disparities among the available data series. This has led to the conclusion that Nigerian policy makers today, as their predecessors 25 years ago, are 'planning without facts' (Mosley, 1991).

Table 11.2 sets out the growth rates of different components of the national economy during the period immediately before and immediately after the implementation of structural adjustment, in relation to the performance of Africa as a whole and a 'control group' of sub-Saharan African countries which did not implement SAPs. Thus, although the performance of the Nigerian economy appears better after the implementation of SAPs and adjustment-based policies, this conclusion also emerges in the group of African countries which did not implement them. This suggests that a great deal of the improvement in the economies both of Nigeria and of other non-

Table 11.2　Growth rates of GDP for particular sectors: 1982–85 and 1986–90

	1982–85	1986–90
Agriculture		
Total	2.6 (1.9)[1]	6.0 (3.6)
Export crops[2]	2.7 (1.4)	10.1 (3.5)
Food crops[3]	2.5 (2.8)	−1.2 (3.8)
Oil production	(...)	(...)
Industry	−2.8 (−4.2)	4.4 (3.6)
Services	−4.0 (−1.6)	3.2 (4.7)
GDP	−2.5 (−1.6)	4.6 (3.7)

Notes
1. Figures in parentheses relate to a combined group of 'non-adjusting' African countries comprising Benin, Cameroon, Ethiopia, Liberia, Sierra Leone, Somalia (this classification follows World Bank, 1990, Table 2.1)
2. 'Export crops' are defined for Nigeria as palm oil, rubber, cotton and cocoa. Central Bank of Nigeria data set is used.
3. 'Food crops' are defined for Nigeria as maize, sorghum, millet, rice, cowpeas, yams, cassava, wheat.

Source:　Mosley (1991).

adjusting African countries was due to extraneous factors, including in particular better weather and an improvement in the world economy. Only a small part of the turn-around in Nigeria was due to the SAP (Mosley, 1991).

Analysis of the period 1981–88 shows that the collapse of oil export income, followed by austerity and adjustment-based measures, have brought about a sharp increase in levels of unemployment, real wage and minimum wages. Both the rural and the urban sector have been badly hit, but the latter has on balance been hit more directly (Tables 11.3–11.6). In this respect, the capacity to gain access to a 'poverty basket', based on cereals and food crops, suggests increasing poverty among low-income groups, although non-wage sources of income, especially in the informal sector, are likely to have assumed greater importance in the urban sector (Jamal, 1986, p. 21).

The rural and the urban poor, who are net purchasers of food, face the possibility of a deterioration in their livelihood. A reduction in the 'rural–urban' gap, following the SAP, may have started to emerge. This, however, needs to be placed in the context of a sharp cutback in state expenditure (including that on agriculture and the social sectors) and rising unemploy-

Table 11.3   Structure of unemployment (December 1983–March 1988)

Period	Unemployment rate (national)	Unemployment rate (rural)	Unemployment rate (urban)
December 1983			7.3
June 1985	4.3	3.0	8.7
June 1986	6.1	6.9	11.0
December 1986	5.3	4.6	9.1
June 1987	6.0	4.9	10.6
December 1987	7.0	6.1	9.8
March 1988	5.1	4.6	7.3

Source: World Bank (1988). Based on Federal Office of Statistics (FOS) Labour Force Survey.

Table 11.4   Index of real wages (1980=100)

Year	Rural	Urban
1980	100	100
1981	89	83
1982	83	80
1983	76	69
1984	52	50
1985	54	50
1986	51	45
1987	47	42

Source: World Bank, (1988).

ment and falling real wages in both sectors, with the urban sector particularly hard hit (Roy, 1990b, p. 57; 1990d, p. 8).

Under the SAP, the rural sector has been of great importance, given its contribution to GDP and employment, and its relationship with other sectors. Devaluation in Nigeria has raised producer prices. Thus, analysis of the crop year 1986–87, in comparison with 1985–86, shows a sharp increase in the real producer prices of specific cash crops including cocoa, cotton and groundnuts, which were previously depressed: by over 300 per cent for

Table 11.5   Index of real household income of key groups, 1980–81 to
*   1986–87 (Rural self-employed in 1980–81=100)*

Group	1980–81	1981–82	1986–87
Rural self-employed	100	103	65
Rural wage earners	178	160	84
All rural households	105	107	74
Urban self-employed	150	124	61
Urban wage earners	203	177	90
All urban households	166	142	71

Source: The World Bank, 1988.

Table 11.6   Minimum wages (average) (Index 1980=100)

1980	100
1981	148
1982	138
1983	115
1984	81
1985	79

Source: Information provided by Jobs and Skill Programme for Africa, International Labour
Organization.

cocoa, 200 per cent for cotton and just under 200 per cent for groundnuts. The regions and particularly the larger farmers producing such crops have tended to gain. Markets for food crops were in existence before the SAP and there has been a weak relationship between prices and output. Factors other than prices, such as technology, inputs and infrastructure, underlie the inability of peasants to respond to price incentives (Roy, 1990b).

Export crops received a boost from adjustment, while the performance of food crops after 1986 deteriorated in spite of rapidly rising food prices over 1986–89 (Mosley, 1991).

Following the SAP, a reflationary budget was put into effect in 1988. However, the budget in 1989 adopted a more austere formulation, placing emphasis on reducing inflation, controlling monetary growth and budget deficit. The 1990 budget was strongly motivated by a desire to seek approval of Western governments. It continued IMF-style programmes which could enable Nigeria to reschedule her external debts (Economist Intelligence Unit, 1990, p. 12). President Babangida pledged that the budget would continue programmes of reform focusing on reducing inflation and containing monetary inflation. The 1990 budget was the first part of the first national rolling plan (1990–92). The objective of the first rolling plan was to 'consolidate the foundations for national development which the SAP has laid' (Economist Intelligence Unit, 1990, pp. 4–5, 12).

The SAP initiated a process of change in Nigeria which can be expected to have a profound influence on her future development. One senior government official has stated emphatically that 'only a military government could have set in train such a tough economic reform programme. Can a civilian government sustain it?' (*Financial Times*, 12 March 1991). There may therefore be a clash between ensuring democracy and implementing harsh economic policies. At the same time there is an urgent need to question whether 'the failure of the political system has led to the politicisation of the military, the commercialization of politics and instability of government' (*Financial Times*, 12 March 1991).

The focus on stabilization policies confirms the fear, expressed in Part 1, that in the 1990s NRNG (neither redistribution nor growth) will prevail in Nigeria.

CONCLUSION

Nigeria's experience suggests that global and domestic economic and socio-political forces shaped development, against a background of colonialism. In the golden age period the economy relied primarily on exports of cash crops and benefited from buoyant global conditions. In contrast to oil-importing developing countries, the debt-led era gave Nigeria access to significant revenues from oil income, stemming from the benefits of membership of OPEC which emerged as a powerful commodity body in third world exports. However, the 'lost decade' brings the collapse in oil prices and its adverse implications in the form of balance of payments deficits and severe problems of debt servicing. Domestic forces, including political instability, have interacted with external forces to shape Nigeria's economy.

In this context, the thinking and strategies behind development show a shift in emphasis from Keynesian concepts in the golden age and debt-led growth era to neo-liberal concepts in the lost decade. This governed the use of state and market forces in guiding economic activity. State power has rested in both indigenous and foreign groups and hence both have influenced the creation and execution of development policies. State-directed planning principles stemmed from Keynesian concepts. However, their practice during the golden age and in the 1970s reveals their inability to take into account socioeconomic constraints. The rise of neo-liberal strategies from the 1980s onwards mirrors the reinforced influence of international institutions.

These approaches shaped development strategies which set out to accomplish goals dominated by growth. There was a failure to combine this with distribution, which was centred more on interregional rather than on intergroup or interclass inequalities. Such goals were virtually abandoned in the 1980s, the focus shifting to repayment of external debts.

The strategies aimed at transforming the economy by action both in the industrial and agricultural sectors, but poverty and employment-based programmes were limited. Nigeria's access to substantial oil revenues in the 1970s should have ensured the success of such approaches. However, the outcome reveals a failure to achieve successful import substitution-based heavy industrialization as a result of a poor technological and managerial base, and domination by multinationals. Thus, diversification of exports, to include industrial goods, failed to materialize. Food production and self-sufficiency aims were not accomplished in spite of Nigeria's 'green revolution', while the 'traditional' agricultural cash crop exports virtually collapsed from the 1970s onwards. Inequality in the rural and urban sectors has been prominent and inter-sectoral inequality was exacerbated in the 1970s by the oil boom. Although the rural–urban gap was reduced in the 1980s, this was in the context of an increase in overall urban unemployment and a decline in urban incomes. Poverty and employment-based strategies catered primarily for inter-ethnic rather than inter-group problems. The shift to adjustment-based policies in the 1980s marks a reversal of development priorities. Nigeria's experience illustrates that development requires both favourable global conditions and effective domestic policies.

REFERENCES: NIGERIAN CASE STUDY

Abba, A. et al. (1985), *The Nigerian Economic Crisis: Causes and Solutions*, Academic Staff Union of Universities of Nigeria, Gaskiya Corporation Ltd, Zaria, Nigeria.

Abdullahi, Y.A. (1983), 'The state and agrarian crisis: rhetoric and substance of Nigerian agricultural development policy', paper presented at The State of the Nigerian Economy, 19–21 October.

Andrae, Gunilla and Beckman, Bjorn (1987), *Industry Goes Farming. The Nigerian Raw Material Crisis and the Case of Textiles and Cotton*, Research Report No. 80, Uppsala, The Scandinavian Institute of African Studies.

Bangura, Y. (1986), 'Structural adjustment and the political question', *Review of African Political Economy*, No. 37, December.

Bangura, Yusuf and Beckman, Bjorn (1989), 'African workers and structural adjustment with a Nigerian case study', paper presented at conference on 'Economic Crisis and Third World Countries: Impact and Response', University of the West Indies, Kingston, Jamaica, 3–6 April.

Bashir, I.L. (1988), 'Economy, society and political process in 20th century Nigeria', *Scandinavian Journal of Development Alternatives*, **7** (4), December.

Beckman, B. (1982), 'Whose state? State and capitalist development in Nigeria', *Review of African Political Economy*, No. 23, January–April.

Beckman, B. (1987), 'Public investment and agrarian transformation in northern Nigeria', in Watts, M. (ed.), *State, Oil and Agriculture in Nigeria*, Institute of International Studies, University of California, Berkeley.

Bienen, H. (1983), *Oil Revenues and Policy Choices in Nigeria*, World Bank Staff Working Papers, No. 592, Washington, USA.

Collier, P. (1988), 'Oil Shocks and Food Security in Nigeria', *International Labour Review*, **127** (6).

Cooke, R.C. (1988), 'Farmers and the state' in Rimmer, D. (ed.), *Rural Transformation in Tropical Africa*, Belhaven, London.

Diejomaoh, V.P. and Anusionwu, E.C. (1981), 'The Structure of Income Inequality in Nigeria: a macro analysis' in Bienen, H. and Diejomoah, V.P. (eds) (1981), *The Political Economy of Income Distribution in Nigeria*, Holmes and Meir Publishers, Inc., New York and London.

Economist Intelligence Unit (1989), *Nigeria Country Profile 1989–90*, London.

Economist Intelligence Unit (1990), *Nigeria Country Report*, No. 1, London.

Economist Intelligence Unit (1991), *Nigeria Country Report*, No. 3, London.

Ekuerhare, B. (1980), 'An appraisal of agricultural policy of Nigeria during the military regime: 1960–1970', paper presented at the Nigerian Economy Society Under the Military, Nigerian Economic Society Annual Conference, 30 April– 3 May.

Ekuerhare, B. (1983), 'Patterns of Nigerian manufacturing industrial growth and import constraints: towards explanation and resolution of the current foreign exchange crisis of the Nigerian economy', paper presented at the Workshop on The State of the Nigerian Economy, Zaria, 19–21 October.

Ekuerhare, B. (1984), 'Recent patterns of accumulation in the Nigerian economy', *Africa Development*, **9** (1).

Fadahunsi, A. (1978), *A Review of Nigeria's Public Sector Industrial Development Policy: 1960–78*, C.S.E.R. Reprint No. 6, Centre for Social and Economic Research, Ahmadu Bello University, Zaria, Nigeria.

Fadahunsi, A. (ed.) (1979), *Planning and Plan Implementation, proceedings of a seminar held at Ilorin, Kwara State, Nigeria, 9–13 August 1976*, Centre for Social and Economic Research, Ahmadu Bello University, Zaria, Nigeria, December.

Fadahunsi, A., Olowononi, G.D. and Roy, Sumit (eds) (1985), *Basic Needs Approach to Development Planning: Proceedings of a Seminar*, Centre for Social and Economic Research, Ahmadu Bello University, Zaria, Nigeria.

Fadahunsi, A. (1986), *The Development Process and Technology. A Case for Resource Based Development Strategy in Nigeria*, Research Report No. 77, The Scandinavian Institute of African Studies, Uppsala.

Fashoyin, Tayo (1984), *Incomes and Inflation in Nigeria*, Longman, Nigeria.

Federal Government of Nigeria (no date), *Structural Adjustment Programme: July 1986–June 1988*, Lagos, Nigeria.

Federal Ministry of National Planning, National Economic Council (NEC) (1983), *Expert Committee Report on The State of the Nigerian Economy*, Lagos, Nigeria.

Federal Office of Statistics, *Annual Abstract of Statistics*, Lagos, various years.

Federal Republic of Nigeria, *Second National Development Plan: 1970–74, Second Progress Report*, The Central Planning Office, Federal Ministry of Economic Development and Reconstruction, Lagos, Nigeria.

Federal Republic of Nigeria, *Third National Development Plan: 1975–80*, Vol. 1, The Central Planning Office, Federal Ministry of Economic Development, Lagos, Nigeria.

Federal Republic of Nigeria, *Second Progress Report on the Third National Development Plan: 1975–80*, The Central Planning Office, Federal Ministry of Economic Development and Reconstruction, Lagos, Nigeria.

Federal Republic of Nigeria (1981), *Fourth National Development Plan: 1981–85*, Vol. 1, The National Planning Office, Federal Ministry of National Planning, Lagos, Nigeria, January.

Federal Republic of Nigeria (1985), *Address to the Nation on the 1986 Budget by Major General Ibrahim Babangida, President, Commander in Chief of the Nigerian Armed Forces, on 31st December*.

Godfrey, Martin (1985), 'Trade and exchange rate policy in Sub-Saharan Africa', in 'Sub-Saharan Africa: Getting the Facts Straight', *Institute of Development Studies Bulletin*, **16** (3), July.

Green, R.H. and Singer, H.W. (1984), 'Sub-Saharan Africa in Depression; the impact on the welfare of children', in R. Jolly and G.A. Cornia (eds), 'The Impact of World Recession On Children', *World Development*, **12** (3).

Hood, M. (1987), 'Africa, the IMF and the World Bank', *African Affairs*, **86** (344), July.

International Labour Organization (1981), *First Things First: the Basic Needs of the People of Nigeria*, International Labour Office, Jobs and Skills Programme for Africa, Addis Ababa.

Jamal, V. (1986), *Oil, Poverty and Inequality in Nigeria*, International Labour Organization, Geneva, Mimeo.

Joseph, R. A. (1978), 'Affluence and underdevelopment; the Nigerian experience', *The Journal of Modern African Studies*, **16** (2).

Kungwai, M. (1983), 'Crisis within agriculture and the crisis of capitalism in Nigeria', paper presented at workshop on State of the Nigerian Economy, Ahmadu Bello University, 19–21 October.

Kwanishie, M. (1983), *Crisis of the Nigerian Economy, Report for Regional Studies Division of the U.N.*, University of Tokyo, Japan, Coordinated by UNITAR, Dakar, Senegal.

Ministry of Agriculture and Natural Resources Joint Planning Committee (1974), *Agricultural Development in Nigeria: 1973–85*, Lagos.

Mosley, Paul and Smith, Lawrence (1989), 'Structural adjustment and agricultural performance in Sub-Saharan Africa 1980–87,' *Journal of International Development*, **1** (3), July.

Mosley, Paul (1991), 'Policy making without facts: an assessment of structural adjustment policies in Nigeria, 1985–1990', paper presented at the Development Studies Association Conference, Swansea, 11–13 September 1991.

Moyo, Nelson P. and Amin, N. (1989), 'The development experience of post-colonial sub-saharan Africa', in *A Dual World Economy*, Wolters-Noordhoff, Rotterdam.

Nyang'oro, J.E. (1986–87), 'The politics of international debt: the case of Africa', *Africa Quarterly*, **26** (1), No. 1.

Ojo, O.J.B. (1988), 'Nigeria: the political economy of dependent industrialization and foreign policy', in Shaw, Timothy M. (ed.), *Newly Industrializing Countries and the Political Economy of South–South Relations*, Macmillan, UK.

Okigbo, P.N.C. (1989), *National Development Planning in Nigeria, 1900–92*, James Curry, London.

Olopoenia, Razaq A. (1987), 'Fiscal policy and economic instability in an oil-dependent economy: the Nigerian experience during the oil boom of the seventies', *Pakistan Journal of Applied Economics*, **6** (1).

Olukoshi, A. and Abdulraheem, T. (1985), 'Nigeria, crisis management under the Buhari administration', *Review of African Political Economy*, December.

Onimode, B. (1979), 'Planning and plan implementation: critique of concepts and methodology', in Fadahunsi, A. (ed.), *Planning and Plan Implementation, Proceedings of a Seminar held at Ilorin, Kwara State, Nigeria, 9–13 August 1976*, Centre for Social and Economic Research, Ahmadu Bello University, Zaria, Nigeria, December.

Onimode, B. (1983), *Imperialism and Underdevelopment in Nigeria*, Macmillan, Nigeria.

Onimode, B. (1988), *A Political Economy of the African Crisis*, Institute for African Alternatives, Zed Books Ltd, London and New Jersey.

Oshikoya, W.T. (1990), 'Balance of payments experience of Nigeria, 1960–1986', *The Journal of Developing Areas*, **25** (1), October.

Oyaide, W.J. (1985), 'Current austerity measures and the implications for Nigeria's economic development', paper presented at international conference on economic crisis, 'Austerity and Privatization in Africa', Ahmadu Bello University, Zaria, Nigeria, 10–17 March.

Ozo-Eson, P.I. (1988), 'External trade structure and Nigeria's current economic crisis', *Scandinavian Journal of Development Alternatives*, **7** (4), December.

Planning and Plan Implementation, *Proceedings of a Seminar held at Ilorin, Kwara State, Nigeria, 9–13 August 1976*, Centre for Social and Economic Research, Ahmadu Bello University, Zaria, Nigeria.

Rimmer, D. (1981), 'Development in Nigeria: an overview', in Bienen, H. and Diejomaoh, V.P. (eds), *The Political Economy of Income Distribution in Nigeria*, Holmes & Meier Publishers, Inc., New York and London.

Rimmer, D. (1985), 'The overvalued currency and over-administered economy of Nigeria', *African Affairs*, **84** (336), July.

Roy, Sumit (1987), 'Basic Needs and development planning in Nigeria', *Science, Technology and Development*, **5** (2), May–July.

Roy, Sumit (1990a), *Agriculture and Technology in Developing Countries: India and Nigeria*, Sage Publications, New Delhi/Newbury Park/London.

Roy, Sumit (1990b), *Agriculture and Adjustment in Nigeria*, Rural Employment Policies Branch, World Employment Programme, International Labour Organization, Geneva, Mimeo, April.

Roy, Sumit (1990c), Book Review of Andrae, G. and Beckman, B., *Industry Goes Farming. The Nigerian Raw Material Crisis and the Case of Textiles and Cotton, 1987*, and Fadahunsi, A., *The Development Process and Technology. A Case for a Resource Based Development Strategy in Nigeria, 1986*, The Scandinavian Institute of African Studies in 'Africa', **60** (3).

Roy, Sumit (1990d), 'Structural adjustment programmes, the economy and the rural sector', *Africa Quarterly*, **30** (1–2).

Scherr, Sara J. (1989), 'Agriculture in an export boom economy: a comparative analysis of policy and performance in Indonesia, Mexico and Nigeria', *World Development*, **17** (4).

Sender, S. and Smith, S. (1984), 'What's right with the Berg Report and what's left of its critics', Institute of Development Studies Discussion Paper 192.

Singh, J. (1983), Special Report on Agriculture, *New Nigerian*, 28 March.

Umo, Joe U. (1991), 'An analysis of Nigeria's trade with special reference to import demand', in Frimpong-Ansah, H. Jonathan, Kanbur, Ravi and Svedburg, Peter (eds), *Trade and Development in Sub-Saharan Africa*, Manchester University Press and Centre for Economic Policy Research.

UNCTAD (1988), *Handbook of International Trade and Development Statistics*.

United Nations Economic Commission for Africa (no date), *African Alternative Framework to Structural Adjustment Programmes for Socio-Economic Recovery and Transformation*.

Usman, Bala (1983), 'The Odama Report and the real causes of the current economic crisis', paper presented at Workshop on The State of the Nigerian Economy, Ahmadu Bello University, Zaria, 19–21 October.

Watts, M. (1987), *State, Oil and Agriculture in Nigeria*, Institute of International Studies, University of California, Berkeley, USA.

World Bank (1985), *Nigeria: Agricultural Sector Memorandum*, **2** (25), February.

World Bank (1988), *The Nigerian Structural Adjustment Programmes: Policies, Impacts, Prospects*, 30 September.

World Bank (1989b), *World Development Report*.

World Bank (1991), *World Development Report*.

Wright, Stephen (1986), *Nigeria: The Dilemmas Ahead: A Political Risk Analysis*, Special Report No. 1072, Economist Intelligence Unit, EIU Publications Ltd, EIU Political Risk Series, London.

12. A Case Study of India

THE THEME

The Indian case illustrates the experience of a relatively protected economy, with an inward-looking focus. This frame determined the response to both unfavourable and favourable global conditions in the three periods.

The influence of Keynesian, Russian and indigenous theories on state planning emerges, but from the 1980s, and in particular the early 1990s, an intensified emphasis on market forces under neo-liberalism is visible. The ways in which these approaches shaped industrial and agricultural strategies, supported by poverty programmes, are described. State-backed import substitution-based heavy industrialization, with minimal support from foreign investors, provides the key thrust. But industrial stagnation from the mid-1960s calls for investigating the constraints on state action. The limits of radical and technological agricultural strategies, in stimulating growth and reducing poverty, and the extent to which socioeconomic obstacles block poverty programmes are described. Within this setting, neo-liberal strategies have gained ground.

This section highlights economic progress in India over the postwar period including growth, savings and investment, external debts and poverty.[1]

By comparison with Nigeria, the Indian economy has been more closed. Exports accounted for 5.9 per cent of GDP and imports for 8.1 per cent of GDP in 1988–89. Between 1950–51 and 1978–79, the underlying trend of the rate of growth of national income was 3.5 per cent per annum, with agricultural production and industrial production at 2.7 per cent and 6.1 per cent respectively. But after allowing for the rising share of investment in national income, this meant a modest 1.1 per cent per annum rise in per capita consumption (Singh, 1986, p. 58). From the mid-1960s to the late 1970s India had settled into a low 3.5 per cent average 'Hindu growth rate'. The record was not entirely dismal. She coped relatively well with the international shocks of the 1970s, not experiencing the illusionary growth of Latin America and Africa in those years, and therefore avoided the hangovers of the 1980s (Eckaus, 1989, p. 173).

The economy shifted to a higher growth path from the mid-1970s onwards; the trend growth between 1976–77 and 1986–87 was 4.4 per cent per annum compared to 3.3 per cent per annum for 1962–63 and 1975–76. The economy's relatively strong performance in the 1980s encouraged the Planning Commission to go for a 6 per cent per annum growth rate target in the Eighth Plan (World Bank, 1989a, p. 2).

In 1987–88 India coped well with a major drought. A relatively small drop in agricultural output and continued high growth in industry and services prevailed (World Bank, 1989a, Chapter 1:1). In 1988/89, buoyed by an excellent monsoon, GDP growth was estimated at about 9 per cent by the government, agricultural output grew sharply and industry continued its strong performance. Higher growth with potential for increasing began to emerge (World Bank, 1989a).

Raising domestic savings, as noted in Part 1, is essential for boosting investment and growth, but is not a sufficient condition. The Indian experience shows that the source of the savings and the ways in which they are used can influence investment.

Over 1950–80 there was a significant increase in the domestic savings rate as a proportion of GDP even though the increase in the level of per capita income has been very modest based on the same set of statistics (Chakravarty, 1984, p. 845). Investment has not matched the high level of savings.

The low level of domestic savings was recognized in the early 1950s. The theoretical literature of the period suggested that the economy would achieve 'self-sustained take-off' when about 12 per cent of GDP as savings was reached. By the mid-1970s the savings rate crossed 20 per cent and reached a record level of 25 per cent in 1978–79. Subsequently, there was a small decrease. The Seventh Plan estimated the savings rate to be 23.1 per cent in 1984–85; this was to be raised to 24.3 per cent by 1989–90. The Committee to Review the Working of the Monetary System, also known as the Chakravarty Committee, was set up. No large-scale changes in the sectoral composition of domestic savings were found. The household sector accounted for the bulk of national savings amounting to 73.7 per cent in 1950–51 rising to 74.3 per cent in 1983–84. The share of the public sector increased marginally from 17.2 per cent in 1950–51 to 18 per cent in 1983–84, while the corporate sector declined from 9.1 per cent to 7.7 per cent (Kurien, 1987, pp. 9–10).

A critical question is the proportion of the households in the economy which account for savings. Given that 40 per cent were below and another 20–30 per cent marginally above the poverty level, 70 to 75 per cent of the households were unlikely to be savers. This finding was supported by a country-wide study in 1975–76, conducted by the National Council of Applied Economic Research, which showed that the share in total household savings of the bottom 70 per cent of the households was only just over 6 per cent, while that of the top 10 per cent was about 68 per cent and of the top 5 per cent alone 50 per cent (Kurien, 1987, pp. 11–12).

India's gross domestic savings as a percentage of the GDP were over 22 per cent in the early 1980s; this was about equal to that of middle- and even some high-income countries. But the high savings rate has not led to a high growth rate because capital–output ratios are rising (Bardhan, 1984).

Changes in sectoral contribution show the extent to which an economy has been transformed. This is shown in Table 12.1. Over 1962–63 to 1985–86 the sectoral shares have been undergoing change, although agriculture still remains important.

Table 12.1   Sectoral shares (%)*

	1962–63	1980–81	1985–86
Agriculture	50.5	38.0	30.5
Industry	20.2	25.8	30.6
Services	29.0	36.2	38.9

* In constant prices
Source: World Bank (1989a), p. 2. Based on Table, 'India: Real GDP Growth Rates and Value Added in Major Sectors'.

The industrial sector went through different phases over the post-independence era. There was relatively sustained expansion up to the mid-1960s with industrial growth of 7.1 per cent between 1951 and 1965. Subsequently, industrial growth slowed down for nearly a decade with a growth rate of only 3.4 per cent between 1965 and 1975. Since the mid-1970s, and particularly more recently, there have been signs of an industrial revival, with a growth rate between 1975 and 1986 of 5.8 per cent (Desai, 1988, p. 5).

Against the background of a higher growth rate in the 1980s, the sectoral growth profile reveals improvement in performance during 1980–81 to 1986–87, compared to 1971–72 to 1979–80. This applied to all the sectors, including mining, manufacturing and electricity generation (Tandon, 1989, pp. 30–32).

Compared with many African and Latin American countries, fluctuations in trade and external debts have not been problematic. However, concern has been voiced in the late 1980s and early 1990s about mounting debts.

India's external debt to GDP ratio at the end of 1984–85 was 17 per cent. This ratio is low compared to most developing countries, while the debt service ratio stood at a modest 15.5 per cent (Joshi and Little, 1987, p. 374).

Recently, however, India's external debts have been increasing. At the close of December 1987, they were as much as $50.4 billion, making her the fifth largest debtor among the developing countries. Outstanding external debts grew by $7 billion or 16 per cent between 1986 (end) and 1987 (end). Borrowings in the international financial markets rose almost twice as fast as total debt in 1987: by $2.7 billion or 31 per cent (*Economic and Political Weekly*, 1989, pp. 216–17).

The World Bank debt tables show that between March 1985 and March 1988 India's total medium- and long-term (MLT) debt, including private non-guaranteed debt, increased from $US25.6 billion to $US40.8 billion. This marks an increase of nearly 60 per cent in three years; MLT is estimated to have increased a further 9.1 per cent in 1988, reaching about $US44 billion in March 1989. Including estimated short-term debt obligations to the IMF, the total debt stock amounted to about $US49.5 billion, excluding non-resident deposits of about $US8.9 billion; the non-concessional component of India's publicly guaranteed MLT debt, excluding IMF, increased from 21 per cent in March 1985 to 30 per cent in March 1988; this increase has hardened the average cost of external debt (World Bank, 1989a, p. 34).

Debt servicing, including interest payments, amortization and IMF repayments and interest, but excluding interest on NRI accounts, amounted to an estimated 27 per cent of current exchange receipts (based on World Bank debt tables) which differ from the Government of India figures because of differences in coverage, exchange rates and timing. This represents a slight reduction from 1987/88's 28 per cent ratio, reflecting an increased growth rate of current receipts; however, the still low ratio of exports to imports (0.65) and to GDP (5.3 per cent) means that India remains vulnerable to rapid increases in import prices or tightening of international capital markets (World Bank, 1989a). In the early 1990s, India started turning to the IMF so as to be able to finance mounting external debts.

The departure of many immigrants from Kuwait, following the recent conflict in the Middle East, has reduced remittances to the home countries. Export growth must increasingly pay for India's rising import bill (World Bank, 1989a, p. 38).

Concern over redistribution, with the objective of alleviating poverty and reducing inequality, has been extensive, but it is essential to distinguish between the rhetorics and the reality. Laudable intentions of abolishing poverty have not been matched by performance. In fact, 'despite India's long period of steady and unprecedented real growth (and partial "modernization") there has been no substantial fall in the proportion of persons in absolute poverty, based upon any plausible and constant definition of those terms; nor in the extent to which, on average, those persons fall short of the poverty line' (Lipton, 1984, p. 475).

Agricultural and industrial development has intensified interregional and interclass inequality. Organized sector workers and middle and large peasants have been gaining at the expense of unorganized sector workers, agricultural labourers and artisans (Desai, 1988, p. 13; Lipton, 1984, p. 478).

The relationship between the trend of agricultural production and the incidence of rural poverty should be an inverse one. But the Indian evidence uncovers a more complex relationship. Until the mid-1970s, agricultural production grew at a higher rate than population growth. The regional distribution of the realized agricultural growth has been highly uneven. There was no significant downward trend in the incidence of rural poverty until the mid-1970s (Singh, 1986, p. 58).

Poverty includes a growing share of landless and wage-dependent households in the poor as a whole. These households account for 37 per cent of the rural population but 46 per cent of the rural poor and well over half in some states; the casual labour market is the main arbiter of the fortunes of this chronically and often desperately poor rural group as well as many of the urban poor (World Bank, 1989a, p. xxix).

Despite recent gains, the number of poor remains very large. The character of poverty has also changed, increasingly concentrated in regions such as the Eastern and Central states which face serious development and financial constraints (World Bank, 1989a, p. 41).

Measures of poverty are subject to significant margins of error and should be treated with caution. Until the late 1970s there was no indication of a downward trend in the proportion living below the poverty line. But the Planning Commission estimates based on the National Sample Survey (NSS) data for 1983–84 suggest a sharp reduction in the proportion of people living below the poverty line from 48.3 per cent in 1977–78 to 37.4 per cent in 1983–84 (Singh, 1986, p. 57). The validity of these data, however, can be questioned. The significant proportion of the population below a 'most austerely defined poverty line' has been of the greatest concern (Singh, 1986, p. 57). In 1987–88 42 per cent of the rural population was below the poverty line (Ghosh, 1991, p. 1369). By minimum nutrition standards the number estimated to be poor was 273 million in 1983–84 (Rao, 1988, p. 2).

Progress has been made since independence in literacy and elementary education: 36.2 per cent of the population in 1981 were literate, compared with 29.5 per cent in 1971 and only 16.7 per cent in 1951. But the majority remain illiterate, while female literacy has lagged behind male, and the same is true of rural in comparison with urban literacy. Scheduled tribes too have been left behind. Public health has fared worse than education. Private expenditure on health was much greater than public expenditure, particularly in rural areas (Lakdawala, 1988, p. 391). Infant mortality is still as high as 105 per 1000 live births (Singh, 1986, p. 57). Very high death rates among under fives in poor, and especially ultra poor households, were even worse in the rural areas. This constituted 'a central pivot of India's poverty problem' (Lipton, 1984, p. 479). Unemployment too has been a serious problem (Rao, 1988, p. 2).

The misery of urban poverty, including its social and economic consequences, is graphically captured in a study of those at 'the bottom of the Urban Order' in Calcutta, one of the largest and most congested cities in the world (Bremen, 1983). Regional dimensions of inequality and poverty have added to the discontent resulting from personal inequalities (Rao, 1988, p. 2).

Indian experience confirms that 'trickle down' has not materialized. The basic needs of the poor and deprived sections of society have not been met, while disparities have widened over the years. Concern over the pattern of distribution of per capita income has led to evolving concepts which can measure a person's physical well being (Karkal and Rajan, 1991).

NOTE

1. India gained independence in 1947. The Indian Plans embrace the First Plan (1951/52–1955/56), the Second Plan (1956/57–1960/61), the Third Plan (1961/62–1965/66), the Fourth Plan (1969–74), the Fifth Plan (1974–79), the Sixth Plan (1980–85) and the Seventh Plan (1985–90).

13. India in the Postwar Period

This section analyses the emergence of development thinking and its impact on moulding development strategies over the postwar period.

Thinking on development is centred on the ways in which Keynesian, Mahalanobis and Russian concepts shaped planning and state intervention. However, from the 1980s onwards, and especially in the early 1990s, the neo-liberal school started exercising influence on policy making. The debate has to be seen in the context of India's relationship with the world economy.

THE DOMESTIC–GLOBAL PARADIGM

This is set against the background of India's colonial and post-colonial socioeconomic structure, which colonial policies had an important role in shaping. The colonial administration was preoccupied with maintenance of law and order, tax collection and defence. These spheres absorbed the bulk of the meagre public revenues. A laissez-faire approach was adopted towards development. Large investments were made in building the railway network in order to ease the movement of raw materials from the hinterland to the ports and meet strategic requirements. They also brought about easier and cheaper access to a wider market. However, public investment in irrigation, roads, education and other development-centred infrastructure was limited. There was little encouragement of indigenous industry. Colonial policies actually brought about the decline and disappearance of India's traditional industry. They failed to make much impact despite greater interest in developmental problems from the 1930s onwards (Vaidyanathan, 1983, p. 947).

The pre-independence period was marked by near stagnation, with growth of aggregate real output during the first half of the twentieth century of less than 2 per cent a year, and per capita output by 0.5 per cent a year or less. The production structure remained virtually unchanged, while the growth of modern manufacturing was probably neutralized by the displacement of traditional crafts, and in any case was not significant enough to make a difference to the overall condition. At independence, the economy was dominated by agriculture, with about 85 per cent of the population living in villages and depending on agriculture and related occupations, using traditional, low productivity techniques (Vaidyanathan, 1983).

India's relative political stability has been a firm base on which to develop. However, in recent years, secessionist, religious and inter-caste conflicts have created uncertainty.

The division of power between the federal (or union) and the state levels, has been constitutionally sanctioned (Hettne, 1988, p. 93). This carries both economic and political implications of development within the individual states. Domestic and external political strife, at particular periods, has created diversions. States including Assam and those in the Punjab, in recent years, have demanded greater autonomy. Inter-caste and religious rivalry have compounded such problems.

Wars create diversions from development goals and deprive the economy of scarce resources. India has had clashes with neighbours: with China in 1962 and three wars with Pakistan since independence, the first two over Pakistan's claim to Kashmir and the third in December 1971, which led to secession from Pakistan of its eastern wing, now Bangladesh. Indian troops have also been sent to Sri Lanka, to oversee a ceasefire agreement between the Tamil Guerillas and the Sri Lankan government. Defence and development models can be mutually supportive (Hettne, 1988, p. 80).

Defence, however, has had a modest, although rising, claim on GDP: 3.1 per cent in 1984–85 and 4.1 per cent in 1986–87. It accounted for 20 per cent of central government expenditure in the 1987–88 budget (Economist Intelligence Unit, 1987, p. 6).

Key features of India's links with the global economy, over the postwar years, can be reviewed in relation to the aims of Bretton Woods (Agarwal, 1987, p. 286). These have been fairly confined, enabling India to minimize the consequences of any adverse external changes. She has also tried to minimize interference by other countries in her domestic and foreign policies.

India established a close relationship with the large international bodies and has been one of the chief recipients of the World Bank's International Development Agency (IDA) loans, which are relatively cheap, with low interest rates and long payback periods. India's bargaining power vis-à-vis the World Bank mirrors her capacity to collaborate with the latter on favourable terms, in comparison with other developing countries. This is illustrated by the experience of India's fertilizer industry. The Indian government had to struggle with the World Bank and multinationals to secure favourable terms (Roy, 1990a, pp. 106–13). In the early 1980s, India took an IMF loan, though only a part of it.

The 'golden age' offered developing countries the opportunity of exploiting buoyant global conditions. In the immediate post-independence period establishing a unified nation and providing an institutional framework preoccupied policy interest. Inflation, coupled with shortages and controls stemming from the Second World War, had to be resolved. Plans set out the frame within which a new India was to be built. India's relationship with the global economy was discussed in the First Five-Year Plan. Confidence was lacking in accelerating exports, which consisted mainly of primary products. Such exports were expected to grow very slowly. Emphasis was placed on domestic investment rather than expansion of exports. Technical assistance was the main form of external help (Agarwal, 1987, p. 288). India's accumulation of sterling balances during the war helped to reduce her need to increase exports.

As stated in Part 1, aid can compensate for any deficiencies in domestic savings. Bilateral and multilateral aid was provided to the newly emerging independent developing countries. This was motivated by both economic and political factors. The USA, for instance, provided India with technical aid, under the Indo-US Technical Cooperation Programme established in 1951. Aid was given to India under the Mutual Security Act and on the grounds of promoting national security by strengthening allies of the USA and developing the LDCs. Fear of communist invasion or takeover increased the incentive to give aid. India's policy of non-alignment, however, inhibited the acceptance of substantial aid under the Mutual Security Act (Agarwal, 1987, p. 289).

Western industrialized countries were reluctant to support India's public sector industries. However, Indo–Soviet economic cooperation strengthened India's bargaining power vis-à-vis Western countries. Following the establishment of a steel plant at Bhilai, the UK and France gave financial and technical help for building steel plants in the public sector in Durgapur and Rourkela. Cooperation was not forthcoming in India's oil-prospecting efforts but she was able to obtain help from the Soviet Union (Agarwal, 1987, pp. 289–90).

Over 1957–58 to 1967–68, still within the golden age period, although considerable growth took place in world trade, India's exports stagnated. A balance of payments crisis, which emerged in 1957–58, as the Second Plan was being implemented, gave rise to a large-scale international effort to supply India with aid. Despite her non-alignment and public sector policies for development, a resolution in the Mutual Security Bill of 1959 fully recognized the importance to US security of successful execution of India's development plans. The inflow of soft aid to carry out the Second and Third Five-Year Plans was substantial. This, however, was offset by wars with China and Pakistan. The problems were compounded by an inadequate supply of food and stagnant exports (Agarwal, 1987, p. 291). India did receive substantial food aid under US PL480. The provision of such aid has often been conditional on India pursuing policies acceptable to the USA (Frankel, 1978, p. 286). For instance, the unprecedented decline in agricultural production of 17 per cent between 1964/65 and 1965/66, following the failure of the monsoons, placed enormous pressure on the Indian government. It was stated in parliament in November 1965 that all government buffer stocks were exhausted. The only alternative was to arrange for substantial imports. In the meantime, the USA had indefinitely suspended all aid to both India and Pakistan, to express displeasure at what she considered to be a waste of scarce resources in an unproductive war. Moreover, the USA refused to sign a fresh long-term agreement with India under PL480 when the agreement expired in August 1965, and adopted a 'short tether' policy of supplying stocks sufficient only to meet requirements a few months at a time, and explicitly tying the continuation of food aid to the adoption by India of policies aimed at increasing agricultural production and curbing population growth (Frankel, 1978, pp. 285–6).

Increases in the price of oil imports in 1973–74 and 1979–80, as emphasized in Part 1, dealt a severe blow to many oil-importing developing countries. However, India was able to withstand the effects of the increased cost of oil imports because of factors including its limited dependence on trade, inflows of foreign exchange, including home remittances from workers overseas, and reductions in oil consumption.

Economic performance was maintained in spite of changes in the world economy. India's growth rate was similar to that in the 1950s and 1960s. Growth in agricultural output reduced dependence on large-scale food aid. An improvement in exports was, however, short-lived.

As mentioned earlier, trade contributed a less significant proportion to India's GDP than in Nigeria. But foreign exchange has been a main constraint on growth and, to that extent, external trade policy is important. Indian economic policy has not until recently treated exports as simply covering the cost of residual import requirements. Her share of world markets has shrunk from 2.4 per cent in 1951/52 to around 0.5 per cent now (the low point was 0.42 per cent in 1980–81) (Economist Intelligence Unit, 1987, p. 41; and 1990–91).

With this inward-looking thrust, India's share of world exports has continued to decline, recording less than 0.5 per cent in 1980 (Agarwal, 1987, pp. 295–6). Her share in the world economy, and particularly among the third world countries, has fallen. This amounted to nearly 2 per cent of world trade in 1950 and was reduced by the early 1980s to a mere 0.5 per cent, making her a marginal trading partner compared with Brazil and/or South Korea. Her position shows that neither the volume nor the relative prices of the products exported have risen significantly over the last 30 years (Patel, 1985, p. 6).

Steps to increase India's exports from the early 1980s onwards have been motivated by the desire to stimulate competition for the domestic inputs at lower international prices. Exports have played a minor role in India's development strategy, mainly providing for the import of capital goods which cannot be domestically produced. Concessional aid was readily available in the 1960s. Aid from the World Bank and the International Development Association helped India to retain her export position (Agarwal, 1987, pp. 296–7). Her focus from the early 1980s on promoting the export sector has to be placed against the background of a relatively depressed global economy, in comparison with the boom years of the 1950s and 1960s.

THE STATE AND DEVELOPMENT

The Indian state has played a major role in shaping and implementing development policies within a 'mixed' economy context. Her experience offers useful insights into the strengths and limits of interventions.

Both public and private ownership have co-existed in India, with direct regulation and indirect influence over private decisions. Indian development can be viewed from different ideological positions, including those which place emphasis on opposition of interests between town and country. In contrast, others put forward the political economy of class opposition based on the Marxian tradition as the main explanation behind the pattern of development (Toye, 1988). Clearly, it is essential to understand more fully the forces which have guided state actions (Baru, 1988; Roy 1990a, pp. 43–5, 86–91). This is not possible in this book but some of the key features can be identified.

The Indian state has been perceived as being 'overdeveloped' at independence as a result of the inheritance of a large bureaucracy, army and legal apparatus from the colonial rulers. It has acquired powers of direct ownership and control in the economy to an extent unparalleled in Indian history, both in the spheres of circulation and production (Bardhan, 1984, pp. 37–8). This cannot be divorced from the social forces underlying the struggle for national freedom, built on ideals including economic development to enhance independence, fulfilment of mass aspirations for a better life and balancing the interests of different regions and classes (Desai, 1988, p. 1). Concern for equity and social justice was a distinctive feature of the national movement for freedom (Singh, 1986, p. 56).

In this context, the class nature of the Indian state has been an important inhibiting factor in bringing about balanced development. The interests of the dominant proprietary classes, including the industrialists, rich farmers and bureaucrats, have constituted stumbling blocks in realizing policy goals of balanced development and equitable distribution (Bardhan, 1984, pp. 37–44).

KEYNES, MAHALANOBIS AND NEO-LIBERALISM

The state, as explained in Part 1, was instrumental in making macroeconomic plans to maximize output and employment, mobilize latent resources and control inflation. Redistributive concerns have been widely debated by Indian planners, but growth has been the main force. The principles of macroeconomic management over the postwar period have stemmed from Keynesian, Russian and indigenous models, based on Mahalanobis. However, in the last decade, market-based, neo-liberal theories have challenged the virtues of state planning.

Planning has been seen as a response to market failure. However, the market mechanism in India was not totally cast aside and replaced by centralized planning. The nationalist movement precluded any drastic departure from a path that accepted private ownership of capital in industry and peasant proprietorship in agriculture. Some of the early attempts at national planning came from the business community. But socialist sentiment was not wholly absent, even in the pre-independence deliberations of the Congress Party and the National Planning Committee that it set up. After independence, 'the logic of a mass democracy led over time to a more vigorous articulation of socialist intent' (Desai, 1988, p. 1).

Part 1 discussed an over-emphasis on physical capital accumulation arising from the Keynesian consensus embodied in the Harrod–Domar formula, in the golden age period of the 1950s and 1960s. In the Indian case, however, there was an attempt to synthesize the three key influences on planning. Economic and political factors shaped post-independence economic policies. Nehru and others took 'imperialism' and 'capitalism' to be the main political and economic obstacles which had to be destroyed through nationalism and socialism. The key thrust of the Indian National Congress and its leaders was political: 'Swaraj' or self-government (Chaudhuri, 1988, pp. 272–3).

The mid-nineteenth century onwards saw Indian nationalists advocating a 'boycott' of British goods as a strategy for reviving Indian industries, which had been adversely affected by British commercial policy in India. This saw the beginning of import substitution for domestic cotton textiles. In 1872, Justice M.G. Ranade popularized the idea of 'swadeshi' which underpinned the preference for goods produced in one's own country. There was a call for the people themselves to provide this protection for India's infant industries through a vigorous 'swadeshi' movement. The refusal to buy foreign goods and the promotion of indigenous industry were intertwined. Indeed, from 1905 onwards the freedom struggle centred on these two aspects of boycott and swadeshi. The political context of 'swadeshi' was 'swaraj' (Dahiya and Singer, 1986, pp. 141–2).

Discussions were dominated by domestic political strategies and tactics, with little time devoted to economic issues. But by the late 1930s, the Congress was contemplating political power. The economic policies which post-independence India should pursue were debated. They were articulated in the proceedings of the National Planning Committee and by Nehru (Chaudhuri, 1988, pp. 272–3).

Nehru and the other Congress socialists discussed the role of imperialism and capitalism. If India achieved political independence but remained within the capitalist nexus, she was not expected to free herself from economic imperialism. On the other hand, political independence was essential to create socialism, for an imperial government would be against the overturning of the capitalist system (Chaudhuri, 1988, p. 275).

The priorities underlying development were established before the Congress assumed power. These were shaped by political factors and not solely through economic calculation (Chaudhuri, 1988, p. 279). But the two most influential Congressmen, Mahatma Gandhi and Jawaharlal Nehru 'saw eye to eye on very few social and economic questions'. Moreover, among the mass of Congress supporters a range of views surfaced on such fundamental issues as socialism versus capitalism, factory industry versus cottage industry, and centralization versus decentralization (Hanson, 1966, p. 28).

Big business, which was influential in Congress policy-making circles, possibly based on the financial support it provided, was suspicious and critical of planning itself. Many Gandhians equated planning with centralized industrialization and showed too little interest in planning. This became critical during discussions of the National Planning Committee (NPC) appointed by Congress in 1938 (Hanson, 1966, p. 28).

Mahalanobis was able to resort to the ideas of postwar Keynesianism, of macroeconomic planning and management, which absorbed the minds of economists and aid donors (Chaudhuri, 1988, p. 280). His one-sector model resembled the Harrod–Domar model but his two-sector model was a product of Soviet experience, based on a 'heavy industry first' strategy. Such industries did materialize in India, based on an import substitution policy, and Indian experience has relevance for other developing countries. Nehru and the Congress socialists were instrumental in encouraging this approach (Chaudhuri, 1988, p. 272).

The first Indian plan models were the two aggregative models associated with the name of Mahalanobis – the one-sector model of 1952 and the two-sector model of 1953. While the one-sector model resembled the Harrod–

Domar model, it did not have any special relationship with the Soviet experience of planning. The two-sector model was a clear account of a strategic approach to planning. The strategy of the two-sector model embodied the 'heavy-industry-first approach pursued by Stalin during the thirties' (Rudra, 1985, pp. 758–9).

Political economists have considered Indian planning to be a variant of the Soviet planning model. This is with reference to the 1950s, and especially the late 1950s. This belief was held by Mahalanobis, who compared his work with that of Feldman, a Russian economist, whose ideas were popularized in the mid-1950s by E.D. Domar (Chakravarty, 1987, p. 13).

The Second Five-Year Plan, which bore the hallmarks of Mahalanobis's influence, mirrored the need to build ahead of demand in the area of capital goods production. The Mahalanobis strategy, which differed from the 'textiles first' strategy of industrial development, adopted by a successful latecomer to industrialization like Japan, was attacked. Mainstream economists felt that the principle of comparative advantage had been broken. Those who were impressed by the Soviet model of industrial development equated the priority given to the capital goods sector with the logic of accumulation laid down by Marx (Chakravarty, 1987, p. 12).

Mahalanobis's models had many limitations. First, the multi-sector models left out some essential aspects of the process of economic development. They ignored natural resource constraints. Second, 'human capital', too, was brushed aside. Unskilled labour did not pose any problems, being an abundant resource, but training of skilled manpower demanded strategic planning. Given the huge investment needs of education and health, the resource allocations and physical targets required careful planning (Rudra, 1985, p. 762).

Observations about education and health were also applicable to a range of other spheres of investment as well as current government expenditures. The models failed to deal endogenously with these aspects including scientific and technological research and explorations for natural resources and means of transport. Investments in these areas constituted in 1965 a quarter of all investments in the country (Rudra, 1985, p. 762).

Indian planning experience has helped to focus attention on the interaction between three main groups of industries: consumer goods, capital goods for producing consumer goods, and capital goods for producing capital goods. How the relationship between these sectors changes over time is at the core of economic growth for a developing country. In a small open economy, given adequate demand, this process may be helped by favourable trading conditions. It would be difficult to fit India into such a frame. Two important limitations have bedevilled Indian planning: first, the prime consumer goods, such as food, have been treated with optimism, and, second, the question of how to obtain resources for public investment, while encouraging the growth of incomes in private hands, has been ignored (Chakravarty, 1987, pp. 15–16). Problems of reduced industrial growth, stemming in part from inadequate resources and limits of fiscal policy to raise resources, started to surface from the mid-1960s. Agricultural growth was also inadequate.

Despite these problems, the models enabled planners to improve their knowledge of the Indian economy and the relationship between planning and institutional change.

NEO-LIBERALISM

The thrust on planning and state intervention dominated India's development strategies. But since the early 1980s, and especially in the early 1990s, neo-liberalism has challenged this approach. Part 1 revealed the context in which neo-liberalism emerged and its weaknesses. It emerged in embryonic form towards the close of Mrs Indira Gandhi's rule but assumed significance in recent years under her son Rajiv Gandhi, who took over the prime ministership after his mother was assassinated in 1984.

The 'new' approach can be identified by a number of distinguishing features. Emphasis is placed on the external sector, in comparison with the domestic operation of the market, and removal of bureaucratic controls.

India has been used as a case study by Deepak Lal, one of the leading supporters of this school, to illustrate the bad effects of a general approach termed 'the dirigiste dogma'. This is defined as the belief that the price mechanism should be supplanted (and not just supplemented); that the gains in efficiency from improved allocation of given resources are quantitatively small; that the case for free trade is not valid in developing countries; and that government control of wages, prices, imports and the distribution of productive assets are necessary for the relief of poverty in developing countries (Toye, 1985, pp. 1–2).

In contrast, the newly industrialized countries, and in particular South Korea, have been seen as models of development with free trade and an absence of government controls (Toye, 1985, pp. 1–2).

The neo-liberal attack has centred on 'the dirigiste system of controls that were set up to legislate planned targets'. This critique interpreted the Indian experience as a 'Stalinist' model of development. Assumptions about India's export prospects were pessimistic: centred on a heavy industry-biased import substitution strategy of industrialization as the main instrument of planning. Planners were more enthusiastic about exercising controls in industry, in comparison with agriculture, which covered a range of producers who were spatially dispersed. The expansion of the public sector to manage the 'commanding heights' of the economy in producing basic goods and infrastructure has been used to contend that extensive state intervention has prevailed (Lal, 1988, p. 24).

Socialism is targeted as fuelling contempt for commerce and businessmen (Lal, 1988, p. 44). Lal argues that '"Socialism" in India has merely provided the excuse for vast extension of the essentially feudal and imperial revenue economy, whose foundations were laid in ancient India, and whose parameters successive conquerers of India have failed to alter' (Lal, 1988, p. 44).

He alleges that Nehru identified socialism with bureaucratic modes of allocation, with its implications for power and patronage exercised by ancient Hindu classes who formed the bureaucracy. This is far-fetched. The equation of 'socialism' with 'controls' shows a limited grasp of the ideology surrounding this concept. The call for dismantling the state, embodied in the 'Permit Raj', to raise the industrial growth rate, is oversimplified. Policies to remove poverty, emanating from this analysis, call for curtailing the role of the state. Attributing poverty to inadequate growth mirrors a somewhat orthodox belief in 'trickle down'.

Despite the unsophisticated nature of Lal's arguments in an age avid for simple political messages, the power of such ideas should not be underrated (Toye, 1985, p. 2).

Terms like 'socialism' were often hollow rhetoric and should not be taken at face value. Moreover, the pursuit of 'socialism' took place within a 'mixed economy' frame. Lal also ignores the nature of state power and its far-reaching implications for shaping and implementing policies.

As explained in Part 1, even in the NICs, which Lal considers as a model for emulation by developing countries, the state has intervened heavily in planning, management and provision of supporting technological infrastructure. The changing global trading environment has also been ignored. The favourable conditions encountered by the NICs in the earlier decades were not retained in the 1980s.

Some of Lal's criticisms, however, on the efficiency of state intervention, need to be explored. These centre on government controls in developing countries. In many cases the state could adopt a less cumbersome and costly way of achieving its objectives, as has been supported by recent research on the Indian system of industrial licensing (Toye, 1985, pp. 3–4). Management of state activities, including public enterprises, should not be ignored. Moreover, the nature of the bureaucracy cannot be assumed to be apolitical and is in fact a main branch of the government and the prevalent political structure (Roy, in press). The state has also rescued a number of private units, including jute mills and mini steel plants, which have failed (Bagchi et al., 1985, p. 12).

Recognition in the 1970s of the limits of growth and the need to adopt policies of growth with redistribution, rather than redistribution from growth, were analysed in Part 1. Such aims stem from visions of social welfare based on equity and social justice. Indian experience illustrates the ways in which such concepts can be adapted.

Concern about redistribution, based on notions of equity and social justice, have accompanied the emphasis on growth and capital accumulation in Indian planning. As discussed earlier, it was a main feature of the pre-independence national movement, and was embodied in India's development plans. Both Gandhi and Nehru had emphasized that political freedom would be meaningful only if it made possible the removal of chronic poverty which afflicted the majority of Indians under colonial rule. The significance of social justice was prominent in the Directive Principles of State Policy enshrined in the Indian Constitution (Singh, 1986, p. 56).

Concern for social justice was elaborated in Article 39 which specified that the state had responsibility for securing a number of requirements. The economic system was not to allow concentration of wealth and means of production (Singh, 1986).

The importance of social justice was further reinforced when parliament adopted in December 1954 'the socialist pattern of society' as the objective of social and economic policy. The Constitution itself was amended in the 1970s. It was proclaimed that India was a 'sovereign socialist secular democratic republic'. Above all, another clause was added to Article 38. The desire to establish equity was made abundantly clear, with responsibility placed on the state (Singh, 1986). However, this assumes that the state is neutral. In reality the propertied classes who have power cannot be expected to sacrifice their interests for the sake of the poor.

Growth of GNP per head shows that though India's performance has been moderate, it has been faster than in the pre-independence period. The Indian State has also succeeded in eliminating famines, expanding higher education and widening technology use. In contrast, failures have been identified in fields which have not received priority, including eradication of endemic undernourishment, illiteracy, and spreading public health (Sen, 1988, p. 1).

In contrast, Chinese and Sri Lankan public action programmes have been massive and successful in terms of spreading literacy, expanding longevity and reducing morbidity and endemic diseases, in spite of not having a much higher GNP per head than India's. Even within India, Kerala has been able to provide many of these services on a regular basis despite being one of the poorest Indian states. This questions arguments which suggest that inadequacy of growth has led to benefits not 'trickling down' (Sen, 1988, pp. 2–3; Dreze and Sen, 1989, pp. 204–25).

DEVELOPMENT STRATEGIES

This section explores the strengths and limitations of the key development strategies which have stemmed from thinking described earlier. India's inward-looking bias was based on extensive state intervention, although from the late 1970s onwards there was a call for curbing the role of the state, and giving more scope to market forces.

Redistribution was recognized as an important objective towards the close of the 'golden age' period, becoming more prominent from the latter part of the 1970s. Import substitution formed the main strategy for stimulating industrialization, while intensive farming in the 1960s became the means for achieving self-sufficiency in food (although at unsatisfactory nutrition levels). The emphasis placed on the agricultural and industrial sectors varied. Special programmes to generate employment and alleviate poverty conceived from the early 1960s onwards, were hampered by sociopolitical constraints.

14. India in the 'Golden Age'

As explained in Part 1, this period ushered in one of the longest and most pronounced booms in world history. This phase favoured the squeezing of the agricultural sector and import substitution-based industrialization policies.

The belief in classical policies was swept away by a new Keynesian consensus on active macroeconomic management by governments with full employment as the primary objective. The conclusion was drawn that nationalist policies should be replaced by rules of conduct devised by international institutions.

India's synthesis of Keynesian, Russian and Mahalanobis-based concepts of macro-planning was analysed earlier. Being among the first developing countries to become independent in the postwar era of decolonization (in 1947), she could profit from the new international understanding created by the Bretton Woods system. Her nationalist movement, in the pre-colonial era, laid the foundation for a state which could aim at self-sufficiency. This subsequently formed the basis of import substitution for industrial goods. She went on to take advantage of aid in the Second and Third Five-Year Plans, including 'soft aid' from the World Bank's International Development Agency (IDA). The public sector also obtained aid from the Soviet Union.

The focus during the first two postwar decades was on growth and capital accumulation, based on inward-looking development. There were shifts and changes in emphasis between agriculture and industry, and land reform and intensive farming methods; the latter did not require changing the agrarian and hence the rural power structure. A 'minimum needs' strategy, close to the 'basic needs' model, emerged in the early 1960s.

Growth has failed, as discussed in Part 1, to 'trickle down'. This was mirrored in India's experience, with the state grappling to enforce equity and social justice. Arduous attempts were made in the rural sector, in the 1950s and early 1960s, to carry out land reforms. These had limited impact. Intensive farming through modern technology, under the 'green revolution', increased self-sufficiency in food but exacerbated regional and class inequalities. Industrial growth stagnated from the mid-1960s onwards, emanating from a fall in public investment and the skewed distribution of income.

There was a shift in emphasis from agriculture in the early part of the period, under the First Plan, to industry under the Second Plan; the latter centred on building an import substitution-based, capital-intensive, industrial sector. Agriculture was again the main focus in the Third Plan, under the 'green revolution' of the 1960s, which set out to modernize food production through intensive cultivation. Subsequently, domestic and external factors, including drought and the temporary suspension of aid, meant temporary suspension of planning.

THE EARLY 1950s

Growth was the centrepiece of development in the early postwar period, although redistributive aims were not abandoned. Inequality was not condoned but continuity of development was emphasized (Vaidyanathan, 1983, p. 953, citing Government of India, *First Five Year Plan*, p. 31).

Role of Agriculture

The 'squeezing' of agriculture for development, discussed in Part 1, is closely linked to the question of the terms of trade between agriculture and industry. The extent to which the terms of trade have favoured agriculture or industry has been passionately debated (Ghosh, 1988).

Planners in the 1950s concentrated on agriculture. Increases in food production and raw materials were linked to industrial growth. Surplus from agriculture had to be mobilized for sustained increase in other sectors (Government of India, *First Five Year Plan*, p. 13). This approach echoed the thinking of the Lewis intersectoral growth model.

The need to establish a just and rational pattern of land ownership and land tenure was an essential precondition for creating greater equality in an agrarian society. 'Radical' theories in the 1950s centred on transforming the latter. The key ingredients were: abolition of intermediaries; tenancy reforms, including security of tenure; ceilings on land holdings; and compilation and updating of records. While some progress has been made, the agrarian structure continues to remain highly unequal (Singh, 1986, p. 63).

Land reforms had limited impact. 'Land to the tiller' was a common slogan during the freedom movement. The zamindari system which conferred legal ownership of land to intermediaries who had little interest in cultivation, was to be abolished. At face value the removal of the zamindari system in the country by the mid-1950s was an important move. However, it failed to have the desired impact. First, the zamindars were paid compensation, which enabled them to maintain their power. Second, vast areas of land could be retained for 'personal' cultivation. Third, those who were 'tenants' had the right to purchase the land under their control by paying capitalized rental values. As a result, ownership of land passed on, not to the actual tillers, but to those who were just below the zamindars. This gave rise to a new proprietary class in the rural areas, who dominated small farmers and agricultural labourers (Kurien, 1987, p. 19).

Harsh political realities thwarted the land reform programmes. Redistribution of land to bring about equality was frustrated. There was stiff resistance from the established urban rich, the emerging industrialists, and prosperous propertied classes in the rural sector. Their power was backed by resources to fight elections and supported by a large majority of legislators, who had strong rural landed interests. In contrast, lack of organization prevented the many landless labourers, tenant farmers and small cultivators from taking effective political action. Fundamental change to the power structure was controlled. Provisions in the constitution limited the scope for making sweeping changes in land distribution and property (Vaidyanathan, 1983, p. 953).

Role of Industry

It was essential in the early 1950s to build some basic industries. These were iron and steel, heavy chemicals, manufacturing and electrical equipment, which all required stepping up of investment (Government of India, *First Five Year Plan*, pp. 13, 31).

The role of political and economic factors in motivating industrialization through import substitution in newly independent developing countries was highlighted in Part 1. Political factors were critical in shaping India's industrialization. Indeed, the struggle for independence was linked to preventing imports (from industrial countries) from destroying local industries. The 'swadeshi' movement of the pre-independence era, discussed earlier, played an important role.

THE LATER 1950s

Policies in the second half of the 1950s marked a shift in emphasis from agriculture to industry, based on the belief that such a thrust could accelerate the rate of growth (Government of India, *Second Five Year Plan*, p. 1)

Role of Industry

Industrialization was closely tied to self-reliance. Imports of capital goods were to be reduced within a limited time through domestic production, which demanded access to natural resources. India was well endowed with iron ore, coal and other natural resources, and so could pursue industrial self-reliance.

The need to depend on multinationals for industrialization has been accepted in most developing countries. India's experience shows how this can be minimized. State support played an important role in bringing this about and was embodied in the Industrial Policy Statement of 6 April 1948. State-sponsored import substitution industrialization, particularly for intermediate, basic and heavy industries, made great headway. Encouragement of indigenous technological strength, lacking in many developing countries, has been of considerable importance in this process.

Import substitution continued to guide industrialization in the Second Plan. The thrust was on investment goods. Prominence was given to heavy and basic industries, under public ownership (Government of India, *Second Five Year Plan*, p. 13). The Mahalanobis model, earlier discussed, formed the basis of this policy.

Choice of modern technology was a main ingredient of this strategy, involving large-scale production and unified control and allocation of resources in key spheres. The state was primarily responsible for planning and setting up of the key industries. This justified partial or full public ownership, control and participation in managing fields where technological factors enabled monopoly of economic power (Government of India, *Second Five Year Plan*, p. 23).

The responsibility of the public and private sectors was enshrined in the Industrial Policy Resolution (1956). A list of 17 industries, including public utilities under Schedule A, was allocated to the spheres of state monopoly, while 12 industries were listed under Schedule B; these were to be progressively acquired by the state but the private sector was also expected to supplement the state's efforts. The remaining industries were to be left to the initiative and enterprise of the private sector (Government of India, *Second Five Year Plan*, pp. 23, 125).

India's domestic capacity for production of key capital goods was essential for rapid and sustained development of the economy. Such goods had a long gestation period and demanded large-scale, highly expensive capital-intensive investment in capacity. This made them unattractive to the private sector. Public ownership was to shape industrial policy and pursue social rather than private profitability (Chaudhuri, 1978, p. 155).

The state's desire to exercise control over industrialization has taken different forms. In contrast to Africa and Latin America, foreign capital and investment has not been prominent in India. However, the Indian state had to compromise by accommodating foreign capital, in the early 1960s, under the Third Plan, primarily because of resource constraints. This was exemplified by industries like chemical fertilizers, where the terms and conditions including obtaining foreign financial support, technology and know-how, and the conditions for the participation of multinationals, had to be relaxed (Roy, 1990a, pp. 85–99, 106–14; Dhar, 1985). Access to resources and technology is essential for such investment. Until the mid-1960s, the Indian state was able to use a combination of taxation, domestic borrowing (at low and often negative real interest rates) and external aid based on concessional terms, to implement industrial growth. But subsequent inability to fall back on such mechanisms for raising resources was one of the main reasons for the fall in the rate of industrial growth. The fall in the level of aid contributed to a fall in public investment (Harris, 1983, pp. 9–10).

Progress in industrial development and diversification was not accompanied by cost reductions, increases in productive efficiency or technological modernity. Members of the bureaucracy exercised considerable power (Rao, 1988, p. 4).

Role of Agriculture

Land reform measures continued to be given special importance because they provided the institutional framework for agricultural development (Government of India, *Second Five Year Plan*, p. 70).

The focus on industrialization and the neglect of agriculture, exemplified by the Second Plan, were severely criticized. A food shortage in the late 1950s and the prevalence of unemployment and inflation justified such attacks (Vaidyanathan, 1983, pp. 955–6). The limitations of the Mahalanobis model, on which the Second Plan was based, accounted for its deficiencies.

THE 1960s

The 1960s illustrate the ways in which plans can be disrupted, even in a relatively protected economy, by economic and political exigencies. The Third Plan took shape against a sharp deterioration of the balance of payments during the late 1950s. This was blamed in part on stagnation of exports, but particularly on the previous liberal import policy. The plan had to face rising foreign exchange deficits and for the first time foreign aid became a feature of the plan projections. The Fourth Plan was shelved till the end of the 1960s.

Growth continued to be the main thrust of development in the Third Plan but plan documents were replete with rhetoric about providing 'the masses of the Indian people the opportunity to lead a good life' (Government of India, *Third Five Year Plan*, p. 1). In contrast to the previous plans, it confronted the problem of raising resources domestically. The capacity to increase savings was critical, with aspirations about increasing employment and reducing inequality. The rhetoric of 'development along socialist lines' was to secure rapid economic growth and employment coupled with equitable distribution (Government of India, *Third Five Year Plan*, p. 4). However, preventing concentration of economic power and creating an equal society was far removed from social and political reality.

The sectoral strategy once again gave prominence to agriculture, which had been neglected in the Second Plan, but the close relationship between agriculture and industry was recognized (Government of India, *Third Five Year Plan*, p. 3).

Emphasis on industrial growth through planned development continued to remain a vital ingredient of policy. The public sector had a key role in setting up industries of basic and strategic importance. However, the relationship between such policies and economic and social progress was not defined. There was an implicit belief in growth through industrialization leading to socioeconomic progress. This was unrealistic in the setting of the Indian political economy (Government of India, *Third Five Year Plan*, p. 3).

Poverty Strategies

Emergence in the 1970s of a basic needs philosophy to combat poverty was analysed in Part 1. A development strategy embodying minimum or basic needs was evolved in India long before 'international organizations such as the ILO and World Bank discovered the "poor" and "basic needs"' (Lakdawala, 1988, pp. 389–90).

India embarked on reducing poverty fairly early in its post-colonial history. The complex nature of poverty and the obstacles faced in dealing with it have gradually surfaced. The zeal to eliminate inequality and injustice started taking concrete shape in the early 1960s. In 1962, the perspective planning division of the Planning Commission, under the leadership of Pitamber Pant, devised a plan for providing a minimum level of living for the entire Indian population by the end of the Sixth Five Year Plan in 1975–76 (Lakdawala, 1988, p. 389). A minimum level of living (poverty line) was defined in terms of the cost of a basket of goods. This consisted of a nutritionally adequate diet, shelter and clothing. Provision of goods and services, such as health and education, by the public sector, was clearly acknowledged. Economists have been basing their research on poverty on this 'poverty line' (Lakdawala, 1988). The role, however, of 'human capital' in increasing productivity and growth, as emphasized in Part 1, was ignored.

Disrupting Development

The laudable goals of development policies can, as explained earlier, be frustrated by domestic and external disruptions. The 'minimum needs' strategy was abandoned because of a combination of factors, including the border war with China in 1962, Prime Minister Nehru's death in 1964, a further war with Pakistan in 1965, a foreign exchange crisis culminating in the devaluation of the rupee in 1966 and two severe droughts during 1966–67. The minimum needs programme was shelved till the 1970s and only taken up again in the Fifth Plan (Lakdawala, 1988, p. 390).

Defence expenditure also absorbed scarce resources earmarked for development. It increased from 2 per cent of net national product before 1962 to around 4 per cent between 1962 and 1972, because of the wars with China and Pakistan. Foreign aid was suspended during the Pakistan war and resumed at a lower level only after the devaluation of the rupee in 1966. Use of devaluation was seen in the mid-1960s as 'a surrender to reactionary capitalist advice stemming from IBRD and AID'. It achieved little in the economic sphere partly because of the disastrous droughts in 1966 and 1967. The suspension and resumption of aid, coupled with its leverage over Indian policies, intensified the popularity of measures to accomplish greater economic independence (Joshi and Little, 1987, p. 372).

Natural disasters too can wreck development programmes. The two consecutive droughts of 1966–67 resulted in significant imports of food, forming about one-third of the import bill. The droughts resulted in interest shifting to agriculture, with calls for increased investment in the sector and a 'green revolution'. India gained access to significant amounts of food aid, although this temporarily undermined her self-confidence.

The droughts and the devaluation made 'nonsense of the projections' leading to the Planning Commission being severely criticized. It lost power and prestige. Despite playing an advisory role its plans have been strongly indicative to central ministries, state governments and even to the cabinet (Joshi and Little, 1987, p. 373).

Resources for development can be diverted towards non-developmental ends. This was evident in the 1960s when there was a shift in priority to national defence. The final years of the 1960s were without long-term planning. The Fourth Plan, originally meant to cover 1965–70, was not implemented and planning was virtually suspended. There were annual plans from 1966 to 1969. A fresh plan was made covering 1969–73 (Vaidyanathan, 1983, pp. 956–7).

Agricultural Technology and Productivity

The original strongly-held belief that technical progress in agriculture would be slower and more difficult than in industry was unfounded, as noted in Part 1.

In this context, India's green revolution, based on biological and mechanical inputs, is a prime example of technological innovation in third world agriculture. It has aroused questions of growth and equity. The programme in the mid-1960s was centred on high yielding varieties (HYVs) of seeds (primarily for wheat and rice), chemical fertilizers, pesticides and controlled irrigation. Mechanical inputs such as tractors and threshers, which had been adopted before the green revolution, could be used along with the new inputs for activities including land preparation (Roy, 1990a pp. 54–60; Byres, 1981, pp. 408–19). The key supporting structures were credit, extension services and price support. Institutions such as the Agricultural Prices Commission offered remunerative prices to farmers.

The green revolution should be seen in the context of renewed emphasis on agriculture in the Third Plan, including state investment in the sector for irrigation and roads.

The green revolution has increased food production and brought about self-sufficiency in food production. However, per capita consumption levels have remained virtually stagnant, while inequality between regions and among different classes of peasants has been intensified (Janvry and Subbarao, 1986, p. 10; Roy, 1990a pp. 196–202; Byres, 1981, pp. 427–31).

Support prices for foodgrains have 'largely benefited the rich farmers in certain selected regions of the country, while the poor have been priced out of buying their necessary consumption requirements' (Rao, 1980, p. 15).

In theory, the 'scale-neutral' quality of the technologies suggests that they can be used by peasants irrespective of the size of their holdings. But in contrast to traditional farm inputs, the new inputs have to be purchased. This made access to modern inputs of key importance in increasing productivity, but access was governed by the relative power of different classes and hence their ability to adopt new technology (Roy, 1990a, pp. 128–37; Byres, 1981, pp. 427–8). Mechanization of farm operations has considerably eroded the employment opportunities of agricultural labourers (Rao, 1980, p. 15). The green revolution has given rise to questions of interregional and interclass equity (Roy, 1990a, pp. 59, 121–4; Byres, 1981, pp. 408–19).

The State and Stagnation

The capacity of the state to carry out its industrialization policies depends on its ability to extract and use resources. As mentioned earlier, industrial growth in India stagnated from the mid-1960s onwards. It recorded 7 per cent per annum between 1956–57 and 1965–66, but the growth rate then started to decline. The fall was marked in certain basic capital goods industries, where between 1965 and 1970 the rate of growth fell to 3.3 per cent per annum (Patnaik, 1979, p. 13). A number of factors caused the stagnation, including: inability of the state to continue raising resources for investment; the structure of demand which created disincentives for industrial production; and the slow rate of growth of agricultural output and incomes (Harris, 1983, pp. 9–31).

The state's inability to fall back on foreign aid and deficit financing, as before the mid-1960s, inhibited public investment. The import substitution industrialization strategy was dealt a severe blow. From the mid-1960s onwards industrial production slowed down. Foreign aid and deficit financing – narrowly defined as borrowings from the Reserve Bank of India only – together accounted for 43 per cent and 42 per cent respectively of total public sector plan outlays in the Second and Third Plans. The additional tax revenues mobilized in these plans came primarily from indirect taxes, the share of which in total tax revenue increased from 61.9 per cent in 1955–56 to 70.7 per cent in 1965–66 (Harris, 1983, p. 10). But foreign aid, as a percentage of GDP, fell from a peak of 3 per cent in 1966–67 to a low level of 0.5 per cent in 1972–73 and 0.6 per cent by the late 1970s (Ahluwalia, 1985, p. 104). The decline in public investment created disincentives for private investment, as a direct relationship existed between public investment and private corporate investment.

Further growth in capital goods industries could only come from an increase in demand, which was not forthcoming (Rangarajan, 1982, p. 590). Despite increases in income from the green revolution, the state failed to raise taxation of the large peasants (Harris, 1983, p. 19).

The close of the golden age period (1950–70) saw the re-emergence of attempts to reformulate development goals and strategies, in the revised Fourth Plan, after the temporary suspension. Long-term objectives were curtailed but the drive towards self-reliance was intensified. The conventional goals of 'growth with stability' and self-reliance were reiterated in the Fourth Five Year Plan (Government of India, *Fourth Five Year Plan*, p. 27). The share of domestic budgetary resources in total resources for the public sector was targeted at 78 per cent compared with 59 per cent in the Third Plan, while external assistance (net of loan repayments but without allowing for interest payments), was to be reduced from 28 per cent in the Third Plan and 36 per cent in the three annual plans to only 17 per cent in the Fourth Plan. Foreign aid, as a percentage of total net investment in the economy in the Fourth Plan, and net of debt servicing (repayments as well as interest) was to be only 8.2 per cent (Government of India, *Fourth Five Year Plan*).

The 'trickle-down' theory of growth has failed in India. 'Social justice' did not accompany increases in agricultural or industrial production (Rao, 1988, p. 11). Special schemes to channel resources to small and marginal farmers and agricultural labour were conceived as compensating for such deficiencies. The schemes, which were experimental, had little impact initially but their coverage was significantly expanded in the 1970s.

15. India in the Era of 'Debt-led Growth'

Development in this decade of debt-led growth was governed by a global rise in oil prices, with many developing countries in Latin America and Africa saddled with external debts and debt-servicing problems. The Indian experience in this decade illustrates the extent to which a relatively closed economy can minimize the consequences of such adverse global conditions and pursue development.

Against the background of efforts to cope with balance of payments problems arising from increased oil-import bills, growth was retained as the key policy, while employment and poverty alleviation programmes were intensified. The strategy of increasing self-sufficiency in food through the green revolution was reinforced, while the state struggled to accelerate industrialization. The Emergency of 1975–77, which temporarily dislocated democracy, provided the context for imposing strict economic discipline.

GLOBAL–DOMESTIC PARADIGM

As explained in Part 1, the assertion of oil power by OPEC in 1973–74 marked a fundamental change in the global economy. This was reinforced in 1979–80. India, in comparison with other oil-importing developing countries, was able to cope more easily with the two large oil price increases in the early and late 1970s, even though the first oil shock of 1973–74 hit India while she was facing economic and political turmoil, exacerbated by the very bad harvest of 1972–73 (Joshi and Little, 1987, p. 373). However, she coped well.

In contrast to other oil-importing developing countries, the deterioration in India's terms of trade, expressed as a proportion of GNP, was small. But the impact on the balance of payments was large. The current account changed from a small surplus of Rs 280 million in 1972–73 to a deficit of Rs 9.6 billion in 1974–75, representing only 1.4 per cent of GDP but 25 per cent of the value of exports (Joshi and Little, 1987, p. 373).

The economy was able to adjust to the external shock in a remarkably short time. From a peak level of Rs 9.6 billion in 1974–75, the balance of payments deficit declined to Rs 5.8 billion in 1975–76 and was converted into a surplus in 1976–77 amounting to 1.3 per cent of GNP. There was no loss of reserves because there was an increase in aid and drawings on the IMF low-conditionality tranches. Subsequently the current account remained in surplus (though declining as a percentage of GDP) until 1979–80 when the economy experienced the second oil shock (Ahluwalia, 1986, pp. 939–40).

Various factors led to this reversal in the state of external payments, including reduction of oil consumption, stimulation of domestic sources of oil and other energy supplies and inflows of external finance. A rapid increase in exports, coupled with slowing-down of import growth, led to an impressive adjustment in the trade account, bolstered by a steady and largely unexpected increase in private remittances (Ahluwalia, 1986, p. 940).

The second oil shock of 1979–80 hit India while she faced another poor harvest. Agricultural production fell by 15 per cent and GDP by over 5 per cent and resulted in a rise in food prices by 8.4 per cent in 1979–80 and a further 11.3 per cent in 1980–81 (Joshi and Little, 1987, p. 374). The current account moved from a surplus of Rs 5.8 billion in 1978–79 to a deficit of Rs 2.02 billion in 1980–81. The second oil shock was greater than the first. The high deficits after 1980–81 had to be covered through recourse to short- to medium-term borrowing (Ahluwalia, 1986, p. 946). India drew Rs 8.15 billion from the IMF Trust Fund and the Compensatory Fund and in November 1981 agreed to a very large extended fund facility arrangement for SDR 5 billion, only 3 billion of which had been used when India terminated the arrangement in May 1984 (Joshi and Little, 1987, p. 374). India used its reserves and resorted to commercial borrowings for the first time but at the close of 1984–85 the external debt to GDP ratio was only 17 per cent, still a low figure compared with most developing countries (Joshi and Little, 1987, p. 374).

DOMESTIC POLITICS AND DEVELOPMENT

Domestic social and political upheavals can disrupt development. The Indian state imposed harsh political conditions to instil economic discipline.

Significant domestic factors impinged on development in this decade. It opened with a record harvest in 1970–71, low inflation (5.1 per cent) and above average growth of GDP (5.6 per cent). Indira Gandhi was victorious in the 1971 elections, and evolved a 'new' policy to tackle the 'old' problems. The slogan of 'Garibi Hatao' or 'remove poverty' was popularized. Mrs Gandhi's popularity increased, following India's victory the same year in the Pakistan/Bangladesh war (Joshi and Little, 1987, p. 373).

Between 1975 and 1977 political life was subjected to stringent controls under a state of emergency. Democratic rights were suspended and thousands of political opponents were imprisoned 'as a move towards authoritarianism prompted by the imperatives of economic development'. A 20-point programme was devised to resolve India's economic problems. The motivations were primarily political (Hettne, 1988, p. 86).

Industrial interests benefited more than the landed interests. In agriculture emphasis was placed on the 'rural poor': implementation of land reforms and liberation of bonded labour. The whole operation possessed an ad hoc quality. A key failure was the family planning programme. Its crude implementation led to Indira Gandhi's downfall in the 1977 election and ushered in the Janata government for a short period (Hettne, 1988, pp. 86–87).

Agriculture–Industry Links

A high rate of growth of agriculture can exert a favourable influence on the rate of growth of industrial production (Chakravarty, 1987, pp. 59–60). This was discussed, in the Nigerian case, in terms of resource-based industrialization with limited foreign exchange. In India, industries linked to agriculture, including fertilizers, pesticides and essential machinery like pumpsets and power tillers, have been leading growth sectors. Control was also to be exercised over lags in production of critical intermediate goods such as steel, cement, coal, railway transport and communication, to prevent bottlenecks in both industrial and agricultural development.

Poverty Strategies

'Trickling down' of growth may demand fairly high rates of growth over a long period. Some economists have attributed the failure of Indian planning to make a significant dent in poverty to inadequate growth. Agricultural performance in particular is crucial for removing poverty. This was discussed in the Draft Fifth Plan, centred on the relationship between the rate of growth and poverty (Government of India, *Draft Fifth Five Year Plan*, p. 7).

The planning phase, 1951–60, saw an overall growth rate trend of only 3.8 per cent while during the next decade, 1961–70, it was only 3.7 per cent, against high rates of population growth. This was put forward in the Draft Fifth Plan as the explanation for low living standards.

In the 1970s, however, as shown in Part 1, growth failed to trickle down in developing countries, in spite of relatively high growth rates. Elimination of poverty became a key objective of Indian development. The first draft of the Fifth Plan emphasized the need to give priority to poverty elimination rather than simply growth, which had ignored the poor. This was seen as a fulfilment of the 'Garibi Hatao' (remove poverty) slogan which Indira Gandhi had coined in 1971. Foreign aid was expected to provide only a small proportion of the total resources for development. Removal of poverty and economic self-reliance were two strategic goals which India had to pursue (Government of India, *Draft Fifth Five Year Plan*, p. 1)

Eliminating poverty through income ceilings and transfer of income from the rich to the poor has been controversial. In India such transfers did not figure in the final draft of the Fifth Plan. A 'minimum needs' programme was devised to improve living standards and reduce regional disparities by establishing a network of basic services and facilities of social consumption in all areas (Rao, 1988, p. 8).

Urgency was lacking in spite of special recognition of the problem by the minimum needs programme. This was either because the programme was new or because of the inability to establish a direct relationship between the programme and productivity. A large reduction was made in actual expenditure on minimum needs: less than Rs 1.6 billion was spent in 1974–79 compared to the allocation of Rs 2.6 billion. The Education Ministry stipulated that finance earmarked for adult education be diverted to higher education (Lakdawala, 1988, p. 393).

Satisfaction of basic needs through a 'minimum needs' programme was integrated more closely in plans over the 1970s. This coincided with the emphasis internationally on the basic needs approach. As indicated in Part 1, basic needs made an impact on development planning from the mid-1970s onwards. But as mentioned earlier, similar concepts were evolved in India in the early 1960s.

16. India in the 'Lost Decade'

The 1980s have been described as a 'lost' decade for development. But it was stated that while this was the case for Latin America and Africa, it was generally less applicable to Asia.

INDIA AND THE ASIAN ECONOMY

Indian experience in the 1980s has to be put in the context of other Asian countries. The latter fall into two groups: first, those dependent primarily on exports of primary commodities and second, others which are exporters of manufactured goods. Sri Lanka and the Philippines, with sizeable agricultural sectors, fall into the first group; Hong Kong and Singapore, with significant manufacturing sectors, fall into the second group.

Transforming economies, in terms of changing the structure of trade and hence the terms of trade, is critically important for development. Thailand, for instance, has been shifting from exporting agricultural to manufactured goods; the contribution of manufacturing industries to GDP has also been rising. Such changes have implications for coping with external debts. The majority of the Asian countries, excluding the Philippines, have not faced adjustment problems as in Africa and Latin America. But many adopted voluntary fiscal and monetary policies to cope with the recessionary tendencies which took shape in the 1970s, minimizing the ill effects (Roy, 1991).

India did not really experience a 'lost decade' in the 1980s. In fact, her rate of growth improved. She did not confront severe indebtedness and was therefore able to confront the adverse consequences of the oil price booms in the 1970s, although the impact of the second oil shock of 1979–80 was more powerful than the first. As explained earlier, although she resorted to an IMF loan in 1980–81, following the second oil crisis, only a part of the loan was taken. Despite borrowings from international capital markets and a fall of non-concessional loans, her debt-servicing burden remained relatively low. But now in the early 1990s she faces worsening debt-servicing problems. This may herald the beginning of a new relationship with international financial agencies and creditors and in turn changes in domestic policies.

Her experience in the 1980s illustrates the ways in which an economy 'cushioned' against unfavourable global conditions can pursue development. Nevertheless, there was enormous pressure on the state to liberalize the economy.

PLANNING AND DEVELOPMENT

The 1980s and early 1990s saw continuation of previous policies and the rise of new ones. Employment generation and reduction of poverty were intensified through special programmes on rural employment and integrated rural development. But alongside these 'liberalization' was encouraged, calling for a reduction in state controls and freeing of imports. Support has also been provided by fiscal measures to stimulate demand for luxury goods among the middle and upper urban income groups. Liberalization has also aimed to accelerate growth. The combined strategies in this period saw a shift in emphasis from state to market forces.

In terms of the near future the government envisages in its Eighth Plan (1990–95) an increase in GDP growth from around 5 per cent in the Seventh Plan to 5.5 per cent in the Eighth Plan. To achieve this a substantial improvement is required in respect of savings, investment and export growth. Plans include a cutback in the public sector by selling off loss-making inessential industries and encouraging private investment in such sectors as power, steel and transport (Economist Intelligence Unit, 1990–91, p. 17).

The extent to which agricultural growth alone can bring about a reduction in rural poverty demands a fuller understanding of the conditions under which agricultural output increases. The policy context (whether an anti-poverty programme prevails) is also important, even in periods of good agricultural performance. The evidence which suggests that the inverse relationship between rural poverty and agricultural performance did not weaken, following the use of modern technology in the late 1960s, also needs to be scrutinized. While substantial numbers of both poor and non-poor cultivating households benefited, smaller but non-negligible subsets also became impoverished (Gaiha, 1987, pp. 584–5).

Policies centred on bringing about growth with special programmes to cope with equity. It was implicit that growth leads to inequality and does not trickle down. There was no attempt to integrate policies to achieve growth with the special equity-based programmes. Industrial growth has improved in the early 1980s, but in comparison with the period after the mid-1960s, the quality of the poverty-based programmes has been unsatisfactory. Moreover, aspects of industrialization may entail environmental costs: illustrated by India's worst industrial accident in December 1984 when a gas leak at the Union Carbide pesticide plant in Bhopal killed at least 2500 and injured 2000 (ICFTU and ICEF, 1985).

LIBERALIZATION STRATEGIES

Liberalization started influencing thinking on development in the 1980s. In the early 1990s, it has been given greater prominence against a background of domestic socioeconomic frictions. The 1990s may bring about a departure from India's traditional state-led policies but this is likely to be shaped by struggle between supporters and opponents of liberalization.

In this frame, an analysis by *The Economist* professes that the only solution for India is complete globalization of her economy, making Indian industry confront world competition and attracting foreign capital to utilize her cheap labour for exports (*The Economist*, 4 May 1991).

The analysis of *The Economist* overlooks the complexity of India's economic and political history. We need to trace the roots of liberalization. It started emerging in the late 1970s under the Janata Party, and subsequently under Indira Gandhi and Rajiv Gandhi in the 1980s. The enthusiasm of some Indian planners for this approach must be understood against a background of shifts and changes in the global economy.

The Janata government (1977–80) encouraged the initial stage of liberalization. This was continued by Indira Gandhi during 1980–84. Rajiv Gandhi made it a priority on coming to power in late 1984. Under this general umbrella a number of changes were introduced, including easing of state controls on the activities of national firms, such as entry into production, decisions on production and expansion, lowering of corporate and personal taxes, and a long-term trade policy substituting tariffs for import restrictions. Some devaluation and lowering of import barriers on selected items were also introduced (Kohli, 1989, pp. 305–6).

Indira and Rajiv Gandhi succeeded in executing some important policy reforms. But the need to build political support tended to slow down liberalization under Rajiv Gandhi. A large-scale shift from a development strategy under state control to a more liberal economy may be problematic within a democratic economy (Kohli, 1989, p. 306). There may also be severe political problems in making drastic changes to the unequal distribution of income.

Neo-liberalism in the 1980s, as explained in Part 1, has been an important influence in advancing stabilization and adjustment. In India, the role of such thinking started gaining prominence in the 1980s and particularly the early 1990s. But, in sharp contrast to other developing countries, including Nigeria, the main motivation was growth (and not repayment of debts and restoration of balance of payments equilibrium). The domestic market was considered to be limited in stimulating growth and this called for an out-ward-looking policy.

The approach was intensified during Mrs Gandhi's last term of office and vigorously pursued by Rajiv Gandhi (Rao, 1988, pp. 8–9). Export-led growth and expansion of market forces in production and consumption decisions were emphasized. The strategy was explicitly articulated in the 1985–86 budget with reductions of controls and more liberal imports of components and technology, confining public investment to the provision of key infrastructural inputs (Patnaik, 1986, p. 1017).

Liberalization was professed to stem from constraints in the Indian economy including inability of the state to mobilize adequate internal resources for investment, limited possibilities of expansion in domestic mass markets for consumption goods and the need to expose industry to international competition (Roy, 1990a, pp. 88–91). Import liberalization was advocated to release competing forces in the economy to relieve excess capacity in the industrial sector, which was attributed to market imperfections rather than deficiencies in demand (Dasgupta, 1987, p. 1601).

The luxury consumption-led growth motivation behind liberalization has been implicitly anti-egalitarian, with production and consumption of durable consumer goods for the rich and upper middle classes (Patnaik, 1986, p. 1017; Rao, 1988, pp. 8, 10).

Liberalizing imports of goods, components and technology for domestic luxury consumption poses questions about the balance of payments, with multinationals exerting a greater hold on the economy. Curbing state intervention can frustrate appropriate research and development, leaving the field to multinationals (Patnaik, 1986, p. 1017). There are also doubts about liberalization stimulating indigenous technological development. This is exemplified by the Marauti car and the construction of colour television sets within India, which have been confined to assembly types of domestic production (Bagchi et al., 1985, pp. 6–15).

Liberalization has led to the manufacture of consumer items demanded by some 100 million of India's present population (of 850 million people). These items include potato chips (in collaboration with Zweifel of Switzerland), numerous soft drinks, junk (quick) food, VCRs and VCPs, 'Barbie dolls', which require not only imported equipment but also continuing imports of components and raw materials (Ghosh, 1991, p. 1369).

In contrast to many developing countries, India has so far maintained its mixed economy frame, with the state retaining the main hold over the economy. This may change dramatically in the 1990s given that she faces mounting external debts. The IMF loan of $1.8 billion in the early 1990s aroused concern about a pervasive external influence on domestic policies.

Liberalization has been seen as a panacea for resolving India's problems but it cannot be divorced from the nature of the Indian state (Roy, in press).

Negotiations over a further loan from the IMF are expected to include demands including deregulation of industry, encouraging foreign investment, reforming the public sector and liberalizing foreign trade regimes (*India Abroad*, 1 March 1991). India's new finance minister has firmly stated that 'there will be no free lunches', a catch-phrase for tight policies as advocated by Milton Friedman. Welfare projects for the poor are not to be sacrificed in the pursuit of growth (*India Abroad*, 28 June 1991). But this seems unlikely, given India's experience of poverty programmes.

Measures under Prime Minister Narasimha Rao in 1991 mirror reinforcement of liberalization. These include devaluation of the rupee, reduction in the budget deficit, loosening control over foreign trade, greater freedom to foreign investment and partial privatization of the public sector. Thus, the rupee was devalued in two stages on 1 and 3 July 1991 against the major currencies by just under 20 per cent. Subsequently, the rupee has been allowed to depreciate further. The finance minister also aims to reduce the fiscal deficit from 9 per cent of GDP to 6.5 per cent. As a result, current expenditure in 1991–92 is being cut by 4.9 per cent in real terms. The cuts in expenditure include those on subsidies, particularly fertilizers, exports and sugar. Defence expenditure has fallen by about 8 per cent in real terms over the previous year. Since the budget was presented, the IMF has asked India to make a cut of another 5 per cent in government expenditure to compensate for the partial restoration of the fertilizer subsidy amounting to Rs 8 billion and its belief that the government had overestimated its revenues from customs duties by Rs 10 billion. The budget raised income tax on companies by 5 per cent while continuing the surcharge of 15 per cent (*Financial Times*, 16 September 1991).

Foreign trade was subjected to several changes in order to eliminate a substantial volume of import licensing and strengthen export incentives. Under a new requirement, imports by companies have been linked to their export performance (*Financial Times*, 16 September 1991).

Approval will be given automatically for direct foreign equity investment of up to 51 per cent for 34 categories of industries. The foreign equity should cover the foreign exchange needed for imported capital goods. A special empowered board has been formed to negotiate with large foreign companies who wish to make long-term investments in India covering several projects (*Financial Times*, 16 September 1991).

The same source also reports that in the public sector the government aims to partially privatize selected public sector units by offering up to 20 per cent of their equity to investment institutions and to workers in the concerns. Government-owned industries are to be given more autonomy and there are to be cuts in the public sector labour force through closure of some companies. Investments by the government in industry will be limited primarily to areas of strategic importance. However, the private sector will not be barred from some of these spheres.

As tariffs account for 50 per cent of the government's revenues, losses from cuts will have to be made by raising direct taxes and excise duties. A committee is also to evaluate the increased use of market mechanisms in allocating credit, recapitalization of the nationalized banks and giving the banks greater autonomy.

India is clearly heading for a change in her economic policies but whether these will be sustained or not is a product of her political economy.

EMPLOYMENT AND POVERTY STRATEGIES

The focus on growth continued, but targeted programmes were devised to increase employment and reduce poverty, among the poor, and particularly those belonging to the scheduled castes and scheduled tribes.

Eliminating poverty within a short period of five years has been acknowledged (Government of India, *Sixth Five Year Plan*, p. 1).

'Minimum needs programmes' have also been enthusiastically embraced in the last decade; the Draft Sixth Plan (1978–83) made greater allocation than the Fifth Plan towards such programmes. Caution was exercised and a ten-year period was envisaged. The revised draft Sixth Plan was more liberal in financial allocation, but did not expect the realization dates for some of the targets within a decade. The Sixth Plan (1980–85), which followed two years later, adopted the same time phase for fulfilling most of the targets. Targets for roads and housing were reduced, while those for drinking water were increased. The health plan was to be completed by 2001 (Lakdawala, 1988, p. 392).

Public provision of goods and services was a key element of the 'minimum needs' strategy. But a substantial proportion of a poor consumer's private budget is allocated to the purchase of basic commodities in the market. This has motivated poverty alleviation projects to increase the productivity and income-earning capacity of the poor. The majority (about 70 per cent) of the population reside in the rural areas and a significant proportion of the rural labour force relies on agriculture for employment. Equity-oriented agricultural development, therefore, coupled with employment generation programmes, can be instrumental in curbing rural poverty (Lakdawala, 1988, pp. 396–7).

The importance of employment and poverty programmes was discussed in Part 1. India's Sixth Plan witnessed a proliferation of such programmes.

Large-scale Indian programmes included the Integrated Rural Development Programme (IRDP), National Rural Employment Programme (NREP) and Rural Landless Employment Guarantee Programme (RLEGP).

The IRDP embraced an ambitious programme for acquiring assets, and was designed to develop self-employment ventures in a range of activities in the rural areas. The target was to cover 15 million beneficiaries at the rate of 600 per block per year, with each block covering several villages. It aimed to diversify the occupational structure and specified that 33 per cent of the beneficiaries covered should be in the secondary and tertiary rural sectors (Singh, 1986, p. 65).

Subsidies and institutional credit were provided by the state to finance the assets provided to the selected households. The capital cost of the assets was subsidized to the extent of 25 per cent for small farmers, 33.3 per cent for marginal farmers, agricultural labourers and rural artisans and 50 per cent for the scheduled tribes (Singh, 1986).

The National Rural Employment Programme (NREP) represents an attempt to provide gainful employment in rural areas to the extent of 300–400 million man days per annum and create durable community assets. In August 1983, a new employment programme called the Rural Landless Employment Guarantee Programme was launched: to provide guarantee of employment for at least one member of every landless household up to 100 days a year and result in the creation of durable assets, which could strengthen the infrastructure of the rural sector (Singh, 1986, pp. 64–5).

The employment and poverty alleviation programmes, initiated during the Sixth Plan, were continued in the Seventh Plan. Acceleration of foodgrain production, increasing employment opportunities and raising productivity levels were the main aims. The plan reiterated aims which had been prominent in previous plans: 'the guiding principles of the Seventh Five Year Plan should continue to be growth, equity and social justice, self reliance, improved efficiency and productivity' (Government of India, *The Approach to the Seventh Five Year Plan*, p. 1).

Employment programmes and their impact on growth and income distribution were discussed in Part 1. The Seventh Plan established more concretely the relationship between productivity and growth. Employment can only be sustained if it is productive and adds to output and incomes on a continuing basis. The aim was to generate productive employment by increasing cropping intensity and extension of new agricultural technology to low-productivity regions and small producers. Rural employment was emphasized through programmes including the NREP, RLEG and IRDP. Effectiveness was to be ensured through better planning, closer monitoring and tighter organization.

The Seventh Plan made it clear that endowment of income-generating assets, for those who lacked them, was the core of employment and anti-poverty programmes. Despite past failures, redistributive land reform and security of tenure for informal tenants were given importance in the anti-poverty package programme.

Shifting of a sizeable section of the rural population from agriculture to the secondary and tertiary sectors was an essential part of the plan; in this context, further development of agro-based industries was of particular significance.

Experience, however, shows that leakages arising from bureaucratic rigidity and corruption have hampered employment and anti-poverty programmes (Sukhatme, 1987, p. 83). Key projects have confronted many problems. This is exemplified by the IRDP which encountered the following problem (Singh, 1986, p. 65):

- complaints about incorrect identification of beneficiaries, with benefits being captured by those who were not so poor;
- misappropriation by bank officials and other local functionaries leading to leakages of subsidy funds; and
- poor income generation, arising from faulty project preparation, lack of effective supervision of credit and failure to provide timely technical assistance to resolve unexpected problems materializing during project implementation.

Nutritional Programmes and Poverty

Malnutrition, particularly in the rural sector, is one of the main dimensions of poverty. Particular groups in the rural sector are likely to be badly hit. For example, a 1981 survey based on 12 communities in six regions of Bihar found that 89 per cent of the landless, most of whom had scheduled caste affiliations, felt they were not getting enough food. Over half suffered from varying degrees of malnutrition; 25 per cent were in the two most vulnerable nutritional categories. Nearly a quarter of those owning a hectare or more of land reported insufficient food and 7–15 per cent of landholding households were judged to be at severe nutritional risk. Similarly surveys in the semi-arid villages routinely monitored by ICRISAT, the Indian Crops Research Institute for Semi-Arid Tropics, have found mean calorie intake among landless labour and small farm households to be substantially lower than among medium and large farm units (World Bank, 1989a, p. 50).

Provision of nutritional programmes has been an important policy to reduce poverty. The state planned to cope with household-level food insecurity, through the public distribution system, food for work programmes and special feeding programmes. The interventions have focused on overcoming shortages in food intake of poor households, seasonal or drought-induced malnutrition and of specific vulnerable groups, such as children (Subbarao, 1987, p. 1).

Food and nutrition interventions, however, have really benefited social groups who were not at nutritional risk, while bypassing critically poor groups, who continue to confront chronic shortfalls as well as severe malnutrition in the drought years (Subbarao, 1987).

Indian experience illuminates the need to avoid untargeted nutrition interventions. Many states have been driven by political rather than economic motivations. Positive developments took place in the 1980s, when both the central government and some state governments introduced innovative, targeted interventions with children and women in vulnerable households obtaining substantial benefits. Their geographical and population coverage has been confined. The lack of any genuine attempts to curb untargeted interventions, in spite of pressure on the budget and adverse macroeconomic effects, have led to programmes bringing about the creation of 'powerful institutional rents which now form a part of electoral politics' (Subbarao, 1987).

Limits of Poverty Strategies

There are two main explanations for the limited impact of employment and poverty alleviation strategies aimed at the poor.

The first explanation suggests that anti-poverty programmes have been unable to reach the poor, because of bad implementation. Lack of political commitment and strong leadership may account for this. The failure of administrative structures to translate programmes and plans into action, coupled with inability to investigate corruption and leakages which divert benefits, have intensified the difficulties (Paul and Subramanian, 1983, p. 350).

The second explanation places the blame on the absence of structural change in society. The poorer sections of the population cannot possibly share equitably in the gains of development unless society is radically restructured. Without such changes, special programmes will only bolster the interests of the rich and powerful (Paul and Subramanian, 1983).

The targets and strategies of development programmes should not be divorced from sociopolitical power relations. Problems facing the poor cannot be measured simply in terms of statistics. The emergence of 'quiet violence' in recent years against the rural poor, and in particular members of the scheduled castes and tribes, mostly concentrated in subsistence agriculture, has aroused deep anxiety (Subramanian, 1989, p. 1). The attempt by Prime Minister V.P. Singh in 1990 to make drastic changes in the condition of the lower castes, by reserving jobs for them, has led to violent protests.

Government programmes over the last fifteen years have been limited in reducing poverty. Alternative options and instruments are required to cope with the changing picture of poverty (World Bank 1989a, p. 43).

The last decade shows a persistence of growth-based policies, centred on liberalization and supplemented by direct attacks on poverty. But there is little hope of fulfilling the basic current plans and the special anti-poverty programmes, unless removal of poverty is integrated with the main planning process. A 'cultural revolution' based on the Gandhian ideals of trusteeship, non-possession or voluntary poverty by the elite has considerable appeal (Singh, 1986, p. 10). The Gandhian approach has always emphasized the need for striking a better balance between man and nature. This has been supported by ecologists and ecologically minded economists, although in the early 1950s such views were felt to lack a coherent foundation (Chakravarty, 1987, p. 8). Keynes himself advocated the limiting of wants, drawing from Gandhian principles, and the stopping of senseless capital accumulation (Singer, 1989). Alas, India's experience over the postwar period shows that major hurdles confront the implementation of such ideas.

CONCLUSION

Indian development emerged within an inward-looking frame, and a fairly stable democratic structure. Hence, adverse global changes created relatively little disruption in the economy, although she was deprived of buoyant global conditions. Thus, in the 1950s and 1960s India did not take advantage of the global boom. But India gained access to bilateral and multilateral aid, although these were influenced by donors' economic and political motivations. In the 1970s in spite of increased oil prices India coped well, supported by inflows of capital and measures directed towards the maintenance of domestic consumption. In the 1980s, external debts did not constitute a major problem and the rate of growth remained relatively high. However, worsening debt problems in the 1990s have forced changes in India's development policies.

Development thinking, rooted in Keynesian, Russian and Mahalanobis' thinking, shaped the emphasis on state planning. However, planning models did not take adequate account of socioeconomic constraints. From the early 1990s the neo-liberal influence, emphasizing market forces, and a more open economy, has been intensified. In this context, access to state power among the major propertied classes has critical implications for shaping policies.

Development strategies, derived from these various schools of development thinking, have attempted to accomplish growth and distribution, by action in the industrial and agricultural sectors, supported by poverty and employment programmes. First, import substitution created an intermediate and capital-based industrialization, with state-backed technology, minimizing dependence on foreign investment. However, from the mid-1960s onwards industrial stagnation emerged because of such factors as the state's inability to raise resources, the skewed pattern of income distribution and slow growth of agricultural output and income. Second, land reforms to reorganize the agrarian structure were thwarted by the power of vested interests. Boosting food production through technology, from the mid-1960s, was effective in increasing self-sufficiency, but regional and class inequalities were exacerbated. Third, socioeconomic constraints blocked poverty programmes. Reduction in defence expenditure, justified on geo-political grounds, could release resources for development. Against this background, the shift to market-based solutions raises major doubts. In essence, India's experience shows that while being relatively protected from the vagaries of the global economy, the quality of domestic policies is critical in stimulating development. Hence, India could benefit from a more buoyant external economy as well as improvements in internal policies.

REFERENCES: INDIAN CASE STUDY

Agarwal, M. (1987), 'India and the world economy', *International Studies*, Vol. 24, No. 4.

Ahluwalia, M.S. (1986), 'Balance of payments adjustment in India: 1970–71 to 1983–84', *World Development*, Vol. 14, No. 8.

Ahluwalia, I.J. (1985), *Industrial Growth in India: Stagnation Since the Mid Sixties*, Oxford University Press, Delhi.

Bagchi, A., Ghosh, A. and Dasgupta, S. (1985), 'Industrial policy and the economy,' *Social Scientist*, Vol. 13, No. 9, September.

Bardhan, P. (1984), *The Political Economy of Development in India*, Basil Blackwell, Oxford.

Baru, S. (1988), 'State and industrialization in a post colonial capitalist economy: the experience of India', *Economic and Political Weekly*, Vol. XXIII, No. 4, 23 January.

Breman, Jan (1983) 'The bottom of the urban order in Asia: impressions of Calcutta', *Development and Change*, Vol. 14, No. 2, April.

Byres, T. (1981), 'The new technology, class formation and class action in the Indian countryside', *The Journal of Peasant Studies*, Vol. 8, No. 2, July.

Chakravarty, S. (1984), 'Aspects of India's development strategy for 1980s', *Economic and Political Weekly*, Vol. XIX, Nos 20 and 21, 19–26 May.

Chakravarty, Sukhamoy (1987), *Development Planning: the Indian Experience*, Clarendon Press, Oxford.

Chaudhuri, P. (1978), 'Problems of industrial development,' in *The Indian Economy: Poverty and Development*, Crosby Lockwood Staples, London.

Chaudhuri, P. (1988), 'The origins of modern India's economic development strategy,' in M. Shepperdson and C. Simmons (eds), *The Indian National Congress and the Political Economy of India: 1805–1985.*

Dahiya, S. and Singer, H.W. (1986), 'The roots of industrialization strategy in India: 1949–56', *Asian Journal of Economics and Social Studies*, Vol. 5, No. 2, April.

Dasgupta, A.K. (1987), 'Keynesian economics and underdeveloped countries again', *Economic and Political Weekly*, Vol. XXII, No. 28, 19 September.

Desai, N. (1988), 'Development Planning', in *National Seminar on India Since Independence*, 26–30 December 1988, Indian Council of Social Science Research, India.

Dhar, B. (1985), 'Technological indigenization and external influence: case of fertilizer industry in India', *Social Scientist*, Vol. 13, No. 3, March.

Dreze, Jean and Sen, Amartya (1989), *Hunger and Public Action*, Clarendon Press, Oxford.

Eckaus, R. (1989), Commentary on 'Global economic prospects: Indian scenario', in *Developing Economies in Transition*, Vol. 2, Country Studies, F. Desmond McCarthy (ed.), World Bank Discussion Papers, Washington.

Economic and Political Weekly (1989), 'Growing reliance on commercial borrowing', Vol. XXIV, No. 5, 4 February, pp. 216–17.

Economist Intelligence Unit (1987), *Country Profile: India, Nepal*, Economist Intelligence Unit, London.

Economist Intelligence Unit (1990–91), *Country Profile: India, Nepal*, Economist Intelligence Unit, London.

Frankel, F.R. (1978), *India's Political Economy, 1947–1977. The Gradual Revolution*, Princeton University Press, New Jersey.

Gaiha, R. (1987), 'Poverty, agricultural growth and prices in rural India – a critique and an extension', *Development and Change*, Vol. 18, No. 4, October.

Ghosh, Jayati (1988), 'Intersectoral terms of trade, agricultural growth and the pattern of demand', *Social Scientist*, Vol. 16, No. 4, April.

Ghosh, A. (1991), 'India: Big World's view of small world', *Economic and Political Weekly*, Vol. XXVI, Nos 22 and 23, 1–8 June.

Government of India, *First Five Year Plan: A Summary: 1951/52–1955/56*, Planning Commission.

Government of India, *Second Five Year Plan: 1956/57–1960/61*, Planning Commission.

Government of India, *Third Five Year Plan: Summary: 1961/62–1965/66*, Planning Commission.

Government of India, *Fourth Five Year Plan: Summary: 1969–74*, Planning Commission.

Government of India, *Draft Fifth Five Year Plan (Draft): 1974–79*, Vol. 1, Planning Commission.

Government of India, *Sixth Five Year Plan: A Summary: 1980–85*, Planning Commission.

Government of India, *The Approach to the Seventh Five Year Plan: 1985–90*, Planning Commission.

Hanson, A.H. (1966), *The Process of Planning: A Study of India's Five Year Plans 1950–1964*, Oxford University Press, London.

Hettne, B. (1988), 'India', in Jerker Carlsson and Timothy M. Shaw (eds), *Newly Industrializing Countries and the Political Economy of South–South Relations*, Macmillan Press, London.

Harris, J. (1983), 'Indian industrialization and the State: a background paper', presented at workshop on State in South Asia, Occasional Paper No. 22, University of East Anglia.

India Abroad (1991), 1 March and 28 June, London.

International Confederation of Free Trade Unions (ICFTU) and International Federation of Chemical, Energy and General Workers Unions (ICEF) (1985), *The Trade Union Report on Bhopal*, July, Geneva.

Janvry, A. De and Subbarao, K. (1986), *Agricultural Price Policy and Income Distribution in India*, Studies in Economic Planning, No. 43, Oxford University Press, Delhi, India.

Joshi, V. and Little, I.M.D. (1987), 'Indian macro economic policies', *Economic and Political Weekly*, Vol. XXII, No. 9, 28 February.

Karkal, M. and Rajan, S.I. (1991), 'Progress in provision of Basic Human Needs in India, 1961–1981', *Economic and Political Weekly*, Vol. XXVI, No. 8, 23 February.

Kohli, A. (1989), 'Politics of economic liberalization in India', *World Development*, Vol.17, No. 3.

Kurien, C.T. (1987), 'Planning and the institutional transformation', *Social Scientist*, Vol. 15, No. 7, July.

Lakdawala, D.T. (1988), 'Planning for Minimum Needs', in Srinivasan, T.N. and Bardhan, P. K. (eds), *Rural Poverty in South Asia*, Oxford University Press, India.

Lal, Deepak (1988), *Economic Growth in India*, Discussion Papers in Economics, Department of Economics, University College, London, January.

Lipton, M. (1984), 'Conditions of poverty groups and impact on Indian economic development and cultural change: the role of labour', *Development and Change*, Vol. 15, No. 4, October.

Patel, S. (1985), *India's Regression in the World Economy*, IDS Discussion Paper, August.

Paul, S. and Subramanian A. (1983), 'Development programmes for the poor: do strategies make a difference?', *Economic and Political Weekly*, 5 March.

Patnaik, P. (1979), 'Industrial development in India since independence', *Social Scientist*, No. 83.

Patnaik, P. (1986), 'New turn in economic policy: context and prospects', *Economic and Political Weekly*, Vol. XXI, No. 23, 7 June.

Rangarajan, C. (1982), 'Industrial growth: another look', *Economic and Political Weekly*, Vol. XVII, Nos 14, 15 and 16, April.

Rao, C.H.H. (1980), 'Aspects of production and technology in the implementation of the Basic Needs Plan', in *The Basic Needs Approach to Indian Planning: Proceedings and Papers of a Seminar in Trivandrum , India, July 21–22, 1980*, Asian Employment Programme, ARTEP, Bangkok.

Rao, V.K.R.V. (1988), 'India since independence: retrospect and prospect', keynote address in ICSSR Seminar 'India Since Independence', India, 26 December.

Roy, Sumit (1990a), *Agriculture and Technology in Developing Countries: India and Nigeria*, Sage Publications, New Delhi/ Newbury Park/ London.

Roy, Sumit (1991), 'Recession, debt and adjustment: some observations from Asia', paper presented at the Department of Politics, University of York, February.

Roy, Sumit, (in press) '"Liberalization" and the Indian economy: myth and reality', in T.V. Sathyamurthy (ed.), *Social Change and Political Discourse in India: Structures of Power, Movements of Resistance*, Oxford University Press, Delhi.

Rudra, A. (1985), 'Planning in India: an evaluation in terms of its models', *Economic and Political Weekly*, Vol. XX, No. 17, 27 April.

Sen, A.K. (1988), 'Indian planning. Lessons and non-lessons', Second Harvard Lecture, Teen Murti Audotorium, New Delhi.

Singer, H.W. (1989), 'When pursuit of surplus ends', *India International Centre Quarterly*, Spring.

Singh, M. (1986), 'The quest for equity in development', *Commerce*, 12 July.

Subbarao, K. (1987), 'Intervention to fill nutrition gaps at the household level: a review of India's experience', paper presented at the IDS RUPAG Seminar, 8 October.

Subramanian, K. (1989), 'Rural violence and public policy: a study of violence against the rural poor in India and its policy implications', Mimeo, IDS, Sussex University.

Sukhatme, P. (1987), 'Poverty and malnutrition', *Economic and Political Weekly*, Vol. XXII, No. 3, 17 January.

Tandon, R. (1989), 'How India is doing: industrial growth and policy interventions in the 1980's,' paper delivered at 9th World Congress of International Economic Association, 28 August–1 September 1989, Athens.

Toye, J. (1985), 'Dirigisme and development economics', *Cambridge Journal of Economics*, Vol. 9, pp. 1–14.

Toye, J. (1988), 'Political economy and the analysis of Indian development', *Modern Asian Studies*, Vol. 22, No. 1.

Vaidyanathan, A. (1983), 'The Indian economy since independence (1947–70)', in Kumar, D. and Desai, Meghnad (eds), *The Cambridge Economic History of India*, Vol. 2, 1757–1970, Cambridge University Press, Cambridge.

World Bank (1989a), *India: Poverty, Employment and Social Services. A World Bank Country Study,* Washington.

17. Lessons of Nigerian and Indian Development

The case studies have focused on development experience since Bretton Woods within the frame of interaction between the global and the domestic economy, based upon the role of development strategies in stimulating growth and reducing poverty. This section explores the major lessons which emerge from the analysis. These need to be adapted to the specific situation of particular developing countries.

The case studies reveal considerable gaps between the theory and the practice of the Bretton Woods institutions.

The International Monetary Fund (IMF) and the World Bank emerge as two key institutions which influence the access of developing countries to finance, for establishing balance of payments equilibrium and providing resources for development. Moreover, their support is conditional on adoption by the recipient of policies stipulated by the agencies. Part 1 revealed the far-reaching implications of the IMF penalizing deficit rather than surplus countries, discarding the original aim of the Bretton Woods system to pressurize the surplus countries.

A democratic political system may enable people to support or oppose decisions on whether to take IMF loans. Thus, the Nigerian military government did ask people to vote on whether or not to take an IMF loan. The wish of the majority to turn down the loan was respected. In fact, however, the government put into practice deflationary policies in line with IMF policies. Nigeria's experience also illustrates the ways in which the World Bank, which was created as a development agency, started playing a major role in initiating adjustment under the Structural Adjustment Programme (1986–88). Curbs on public expenditure, privatization and devaluation were the major thrusts.

It may be even more difficult for smaller economies, dependent primarily on agricultural commodities and raw materials, to bargain forcefully with international financial and aid institutions.

In a relatively protected economy with limited dependence on trade, such as India, the impact of global changes may be minimized. But recent events in the 1990s reveal that in spite of this, rising external debts may erode any bargaining strength vis-à-vis international financial institutions. Thus, India's acceptance of IMF loans in the 1990s was closely related to the adoption of deflationary measures. But India's relatively strong domestic economy can still enable her to fall back on domestic resources to exercise some autonomy over development policies. This choice may not be open to smaller and less technologically advanced countries. Yet other countries have managed to combine an open posture, with an avoidance of balance of payments difficulties and the imposed adjustment which they imply – given the distortion of the Bretton Woods system, described in Part 1, towards one-sided adjustment by debtor countries.

The case studies suggest shifts in development thinking, with a diminished role for the state and an enhanced role for the market, for both outward- and inward-looking developing countries. They show that in an economy where foreign trade is important, the global market conditions may have to be accepted. A buoyant and stable global economy can be beneficial not only to such economies but also to those like India which have placed emphasis on the domestic economy for development. Thus, the scope for combining outward- and inward-looking development should be explored.

Of course, the trade structure, including the terms of trade and balance of payments, is more relevant to a country like Nigeria than to India, although both are large countries and hence can gain from scale economies. Nigeria's case demonstrates the importance of developing countries consolidating their position through collective action based on OPEC. But the relatively short-lived power of the latter does suggest that it is essential for developing countries to utilize more fully, and creatively, the resources which may be available. Moreover, even under favourable terms of trade, as in the oil boom era in Nigeria, the quality of domestic policies is critical for stimulating development.

The three periods throw light on the ways in which changes in the global conditions can have far-reaching economic implications. In Nigeria, the golden age shows that in spite of a global boom, poor infrastructure and technology prevented the country from taking more advantage of the boom. Such problems can inhibit the capacity to develop import substitution as well as export-oriented industries. The second period, the 1970s, shows the gains from commodity power. For Nigeria, this era was clearly not one of 'debt-led' growth, but the seeds of deeper problems were being sown: Nigeria was accumulating debts in the 1970s, although the debt-service ratio was low. It was only in the 1980s that the futility of over-optimistic price projections for developing country exports became clear. Inability to transform the economy in the 1970s characterized an era of 'lost opportunity'.

India's more protected structure indicates the limits this imposes on taking advantage of global booms, as in the golden age. But ability to resort to bilateral and multilateral aid, as India did in this period, may support development, although the major motivation of the donors may be not only economic but also political. In the context of increased competition for aid between developing countries and eastern European countries, the bargaining power of developing countries may be severely curtailed.

India's response to the oil price increases in the 1970s exemplifies how a protected economy can minimize the impact of adverse global changes. But even such economies may not be immune to such changes. Thus, in the absence of inflows of foreign exchange, as applied in India's case in this period, balance of payments deficit problems may emerge.

The case studies show clearly the shift in emphasis from state- to market-based policies, rooted in changes in the influence of Keynesian and neo-liberal concepts respectively. The viability of the latter in bringing about sustainable development and alleviating poverty still needs to be addressed.

The Nigerian experience in the 1980s illustrates the ways in which neo-liberal thinking moulded policies which centred on debt repayment, while unemployment and poverty were aggravated. This was less marked in the Indian economy but her experience in the 1990s provides evidence of the impact of external pressures to curb state-directed policies and emphasize market orientation.

The Indian case shows the ways in which Keynesian models can be integrated with indigenous and centrally planned models, and the limitations of such models in incorporating socioeconomic constraints. The Nigerian case throws light on the risks of mechanical imposition of Keynesian models without a fuller recognition of the role of 'human capital'. Moreover, raising the rate of savings is not a sufficient condition for stimulating investment: as witnessed in the Indian case. Thus increasing the rate of savings is a necessary, but not sufficient condition for investment, and hence growth.

The importance of the source of the savings and the capacity of the state to exercise control over them also emerges from the Indian case. Both countries reflect the risks of underestimating the importance of the relationship between investment and 'human capital', including nutrition, health and education. The state may have to play a major role given the unlikelihood of adequate investment from the private sector in the area of human capital.

The specific strategies in the two case study countries for the industrial and agricultural sectors, coupled with supporting strategies to resolve poverty, yield useful insights.

Import substitution-based industrialization strategies to accomplish growth and self-reliance have been prominent in many developing countries. Such thrusts need to be understood against the colonial history of many developing countries. Political factors may intensify the urge to implement import substitution.

In the post-independence period, India set out to establish key industries, with extensive state intervention, to minimize dependence on the private sector and foreign capital. This inward focus, within the industrial sector, inhibited India's capacity to take advantage of the positive global environment in the golden age period. But such a policy may be justified if a strong and efficient industrial sector, with a capital goods base, can be built in the medium to long run. While the Indian state built a sizeable industrial sector, the planning models failed to place adequate emphasis on human capital. State support for technology emerged as a key factor but the experience indicates that shortage of domestic resources and technology may necessitate collaboration with foreign capital, and on unequal terms. This is illustrated by India's negotiations with multinationals and the World Bank in building fertilizer plants.

Export-led growth emanating from import substitution, a policy which India has considered more fully recently, can be seen as a delayed response, with present global conditions being less favourable in comparison with the golden age.

The Nigerian experience, in contrast, typifies the constraints on successful import substitution-based industrialization and shift of emphasis from agricultural or mineral to industrial exports. Indian experience shows clearly that in spite of access to finance, absence of indigenous technology and management may force dependence on foreign multinationals. This implies reduced scope for developing import substitution-, or export-based industries. A potentially large domestic market, as in Nigeria and India, may not be available in smaller economies, and hence they may find it more difficult to establish economies of scale. Other countries may attach less importance to self-reliance, confident of their ability to become equal partners in the global market. This is dependent on global trading arrangements and access of developing countries to the markets of the developed world.

In the agricultural sector, the Indian case shows that sociopolitical factors may block the agrarian reforms necessary to create conditions for stimulating productivity. But Indian experience also illustrates that the state can support technology to boost food production and self-sufficiency by planning agricultural research, providing technology, and ensuring remunerative output prices. Yet per capita food consumption may fail to increase and inequality, interregional and interclass, could be intensified (Roy, 1990).

The scope of boosting food production through technology may be constrained by a lack of necessary prerequisites: in Nigeria there was a weak agricultural research base, an unintegrated supply system for technology inputs, an absence of a domestic manufacturing base for technology, and inadequate price support for crops. There is also a need to assess the extent to which cultivation of food and cash crops is complementary or competitive, taking into account short- and long-run development goals. In the long run new forms of increasing agricultural productivity, including biotechnology, need to be embraced (Roy, 1990).

The limits of growth 'trickling down' to the majority emerge from the case studies but the experience of special strategies, including employment and poverty programmes, to compensate for this, also reveals many weaknesses.

While state action to eliminate famine and provide higher education is shown to have been effective in India, the execution of employment and poverty programmes illustrates the need to recognize socioeconomic and political obstacles and find ways of overcoming them.

The Nigerian case shows how planning placed more emphasis on growth than distribution, with the latter focusing primarily on interregional and ethnic concerns. This may be replicated in other developing countries, with multi-ethnic communities, who may compete fiercely for resources. The lack of adequate poverty and employment programmes, as in Nigeria, reduced the possibility of resolving inequality and satisfying basic needs.

The two case studies highlight the complementarity between agricultural and industrial strategies. This is closely related to the choice of technology, the scope for building industries with local skills and raw materials, employment prospects and decentralization of programmes. For small economies such strategies may ease the frictions of industrial growth, using agricultural-based and other domestic resources, in contrast to pursuing heavy industrialization. Both countries also show that military or defence expenditure, to fight internal or external threats, can divert from development.

Looking towards the 1990s, some key problems need to be discussed more fully: the international and domestic context of development, the role of neo-liberal approaches in laying the foundations for solid and sustained growth, and the choice of effective strategies in key sectors.

The case studies throw light on the World Bank's view that the prospects for developing countries are less determined by the international context than by their domestic policies. The Nigerian and Indian case studies suggest that solutions to development problems cannot be derived from an exclusive focus on global or domestic solutions but require a combination of both. Hence, to argue that the international context is less important than domestic policies is not meaningful.

A major lesson of the Nigerian experience is that developing countries can join forces to improve the terms of trade for their commodities and hence increase their bargaining power. Oil, in the Nigerian case, did not have close substitutes. But her experience illustrates that developing countries may be able to exercise commodity power over a limited period. This demands avoiding over-optimistic projections of expected prices for their commodities. Nigeria's planning collapsed in the 1980s and there were shortfalls even in the 1970s due to such over-optimistic projections. Thus the search for fair and stable prices for the commodities exported by developing countries must continue unabated.

As explained in Part 1, a reformed Bretton Woods system is required, which can seek ways of making collective solutions to improve the exports of developing countries within existing trading structures. The experience of OPEC, and its gains for Nigeria, holds useful lessons for developing commodity power which may strengthen the bargaining power of developing countries.

Trade can certainly be valuable for developing countries if it is on good terms and the terms of trade are favourable, but it may have little value if it is on deteriorating terms of trade. Existing global institutions are unlikely to serve the interests of developing countries (Singer, 1991). While it is essential for an open developing economy to have a strong trading position, this by itself is unlikely to be sufficient to ensure development. In spite of the 'golden opportunity' in the 1970s Nigeria failed to transform her economy. The sharp fall in the price of oil exports exposed the persistence of deeper problems, with Nigeria falling into the 'debt trap' of the 1980s.

India's experience shows that economies which are relatively protected can fall back on the domestic sector to stimulate development. However this may deprive them of possible gains from trade under buoyant global conditions as in the golden age. But the advisability of outward-looking strategies cannot be divorced from the global conditions prevailing in the 1990s which are less favourable than in the golden age era.

The case studies suggest that there are considerable doubts about neo-liberal thinking laying the foundations of future solid and sustainable growth. Nigeria's case shows a domination by neo-liberal thinking with the military government accommodating to the demands of external institutions, including the World Bank, even before formal adjustment policies were adopted. The approach centred on debt repayment and marked a departure from pursuing goals of growth and distribution. India highlights the accommodation of neo-liberal thinking within an economy which has been increasingly under pressure to expose itself to both domestic and global market forces. Privatization, liberalization and devaluation, herald a major shift in policy. It is however essential to investigate factors which have frustrated state policies, including falling investments in industry and the persistence of inequality and poverty. Such problems may be shelved because of India's gradual accommodation of market policies.

In different ways, both cases suggest that adjustment programmes, stemming from neo-liberal thinking, have to be rethought and linked to development and not simply debt repayment.

The debate on the virtues of the neo-liberal approach cannot be divorced from analysing more closely the quality of state actions. Thus, it has often been implicitly assumed that the state is 'neutral'. But the myth of the 'neutral' state in developing countries is placed in doubt by the case studies. The central question should focus on who has access to state power, and its use for particular or general interests. Current debates on understanding more fully the interaction between the state and the market must be conducted in this frame (see for example World Bank (1991) for an analysis of the role of the state and the need to adopt a 'market-friendly' approach in developing countries).

On a broader front it is essential to look more critically in the 1990s at development goals and strategies. An obsession with growth has been prominent in many studies but the costs of blind pursuit, including environmental cost, are emerging. There is also an urgent need to abandon the rhetoric of growth with distribution, with the latter playing a secondary role. For instance, Indian poverty programmes show the gulf between planning and the rural and urban poor. In a federal state structure, exemplified by Nigeria and India, there are likely to be considerable problems, but each developing country needs to evolve its own methods of reconciling national and sectional, including ethnic and cultural, conflicts.

In terms of strategies, the Nigerian and Indian experiences yield important lessons for transforming a developing economy, based upon attempts to bring about a shift from an agricultural to an industrial economy.

Taking the Indian industrial experience, it emerges that the state can play a major role through direct participation in production and collaboration with the private sector. However there is a need in industrial and trade policies to distinguish between the production of consumer goods and capital goods. Moreover constraints on the state, including inability to intensify policies to raise taxation, may block such aims. The scope of developing such industries into export industries may be considerable, but only under favourable global conditions. The South-East Asian countries developed their exports under more favourable conditions than would confront the South Asian countries today.

The linkage between the agricultural and the industrial sector may create new opportunities for development. In this respect, financing development through cash crops, which may be subject to falling terms of trade, raises critical problems. If this is the basis of development, as was the case in Nigeria, developing countries may be exposed to considerable risk and uncertainty in transforming their economy. Indian experience shows that technology can increase agricultural productivity, minimizing dependence on imports of food. But the role of technology needs to be combined with other measures including land reform and increased public investment in irrigation and infrastructure.

The Nigerian state's experience suggests the need for closer incorporation of equity, especially given the severe impact of adjustment programmes on employment and poverty. The Indian employment and poverty programmes reveal the need for careful planning and the need to overcome economic and sociopolitical obstacles.

In essence, the case studies call for a re-assessment of the thinking and strategies behind development. Above all, it is necessary to envisage another attempt, as in 1943–45, to create a 'Brave New World'. As we learned from the lessons of the 1930s and the World War, so we must today learn the lessons of the 'lost decade' and restore a second golden age. The revitalization of Bretton Woods, in the context of closer integration between global and domestic development policies, is an essential ingredient in this endeavour.

PART 3

The 1990s

18. On to Fortune or Bound in Miseries?

> *There is a tide in the affairs of men*
> *Which, taken at the flood, leads on to fortune;*
> *Omitted, all the voyage of their life*
> *Is bound in shallows and in miseries.*

William Shakespeare, *Julius Caesar*

Parts 1 and 2 have looked at global and domestic development policies since 1945 and the lessons which emerge. What conclusions can we draw for the decade ahead? We have described the 1980s as a lost decade for a large part of the Third World, especially Africa and Latin America. At the time of writing, two years into the 1990s, the problems which have caused the troubles of the lost decade are still largely with us. The debt crisis has been contained but not resolved; commodity prices are even lower – in fact the lowest since the Great Depression of the 1930s – and terms of trade for developing countries have become even more unfavourable. Moreover, the growth rate of industrial countries has remained sluggish and ambitions for the next decade are limited to a 2–3 per cent growth target, not enough to restore the industrial countries as the engines of growth of the world economy which they were during the golden age; there is still no sign of effective macroeconomic global management; and there is no genuine democratically shared global consensus for North–South cooperation.

But it is not all a tale of woe. There are bright spots: East and South-East Asia is one such bright spot; the large-scale perverse capital transfers out of developing countries show signs of disappearing and private capital flows show some signs of reviving. All the same, the best that we can realistically hope for is that the 1990s will become a decade of rehabilitation, of repairing the ravages of the 1980s to enable us to resume in the next century the growth path of the previous decades – and this time, it is hoped, more solidly based than the debt-led growth of the 1970s.

Even this limited objective presents a formidable task. The first thing to realize is the tremendous devastation which the ten years of the debt crisis (dating it from the Mexican moratorium in 1982) have wrought upon the developing countries. Compared with where they would have been had they continued the GDP growth rate of 1965–80, the developing countries have lost income during the past decade as follows: low-income countries other than China and India 35 per cent of GDP; lower middle-income countries 39 per cent, upper middle-income countries 23 per cent; sub-Saharan Africa 40 per cent; Latin America and the Caribbean 45 per cent; the severely indebted countries also 45 per cent. These would be the jumps in income required to bring the Third World back to the 1965–80 growth line. In manufacturing – still the flagship of economic development – the cumulative setbacks have been even more severe: 32 per cent for the low-income countries other than India and China; 53 per cent for the lower middle-income countries; no less than 85 per cent for sub-Saharan Africa; 57 per cent for Latin America and the Caribbean. Only the upper middle-income countries have managed to keep this cumulative loss to a relatively modest level of 10 per cent.

Not all of this economic devastation (compared with 1965–80) is due to the debt crisis. The industrialized OECD countries have also had their set-backs but with a cumulative setback of 7 per cent for GDP and only 4 per cent for manufacturing these setbacks seem minimal compared with those of the Third World and could easily be made up in the next ten years by better economic management on behalf of the G7 and by restoring the growth objective to a more equal place relative to control of inflation – more of Keynes and less of Milton Friedman!

By contrast, to return the third world countries during the next decade back to the 1965–80 line, so as to make up for the cumulative loss during the 1980s, would require nothing less than a miracle. GDP of low-income countries would have to grow by 8.5 per cent per annum; lower middle-income countries by 9.4 per cent per annum; upper middle-income countries by 7.9 per cent per annum; sub-Saharan Africa by 8.8 per cent per annum; Latin America and the Caribbean by 10.5 per cent per annum; and the severely indebted countries also by 10.5 per cent per annum. Failing a big sustained Marshall Plan fed from the 'peace dividend' (see below), the task is impossible (except perhaps for the upper middle-income countries). The only reasonable conclusion is that if we ever at any point in the future are to get back to the interrupted 1965–80 line, it will take very much longer than a decade. The job may have to be spread out over 30–40 years at least. So we will be walking in the shadow of the debt crisis for a generation or more, even if the debts were wiped out tomorrow. It will be a long run and 'in the long run we are all dead'.

In spite of the much-vaunted 'outward orientation' achieved during the 1980s, it is true even in the case of trade that arrears have to be made up. The rate of growth of exports of low-income countries other than China and India fell from 5.9 per cent per annum in 1965–80 to 0.5 per cent in 1980–88; their exports would have to increase by no less than 11.3 per cent per annum to come back again to the 1965–80 growth line. For sub-Saharan Africa the figures are even worse. In the case of the lower middle-income countries, the impact of outward orientation on export volume has been minimal, from growth at 5.8 per cent in 1965–80 to 6.0 per cent in 1980–88. It is only in the case of upper middle-income countries and of Latin America that there has been a visible shift to outward orientation reflected in the volume of exports. And these figures relate to the *volume* of exports and therefore do not reflect the deterioration of terms of trade which has occurred not only for the primary commodity exports but also for the manufactured exports of developing countries (see Sarkar and Singer, 1991). Nor do they show the import strangulation – directly related to the cuts in investment already noted. The volume of imports of low-income countries other than China and India has *fallen* at the rate of 3.2 per cent in the 1980s after rising by 4.5 per cent per annum in 1965–80. They would have to rise by no less than 12.2 per cent per annum in the next decade to make up for this shortfall. For the severely indebted countries as a whole, as well as for Latin America and the Caribbean and for sub-Saharan Africa, this downward shift and shortfall is even greater.

It is noteworthy that, while the OECD members also showed a drop in their growth of exports (some of it explained by the import strangulation in developing countries), they were able to increase the growth rate in the volume of their imports (from 4.2 per cent to 5.1 per cent), largely due to their improved terms of trade – the counterpart of the deteriorated terms of trade of third world countries.

As against this, the neo-liberal counter-revolutionaries which today control many of the strategic development positions will argue that this is a false calculation based on excessively static assumptions. They argue that many developing countries have improved the quality of their policies through structural adjustment programmes and thus 'laid the foundations for subsequent sustainable growth', in a favourite phrase of this school. In this picture of the world, the past decade was a period of necessary consolidation, of *reculer pour mieux sauter*. Perhaps so; only the future can tell, although our case studies – particularly the Nigerian case – throw some doubt on this. If this view is correct, and if the third world countries are really in better shape now for subsequent growth, then perhaps catching up with the 1965–80 line is not impossible, at least gradually in the course of time. The potential of the peace dividend, if constructively used for development, will be discussed later in this chapter.

But there is also the opposite view, i.e. that what has happened in the past decade, far from 'laying the foundations of subsequent growth' has done exactly the opposite: it has *destroyed* the foundations for subsequent growth. This view can find support from the particularly heavy decline of investment in the indebted countries and third world countries generally. Investment has declined even more than GNP, i.e. it has declined as a proportion of GNP. Physical capital investment is not the only – perhaps not the main – source of growth, but it is an important determinant of future growth. Gross domestic investment in the severely indebted countries, after growing by 8.4 per cent per annum in 1965–80, has over the past decade *declined* by 3.1 per cent per annum. This is a swing, in the direction of decline, of 11.5 per cent, or no less than 65 per cent cumulatively by the end of the decade. This means that the volume of investment in these countries over the next decade would have to be almost treble that of the last decade in order to bring it back to the 1965–80 line. The corresponding figures for sub-Saharan Africa and for Latin America are equally bad or worse. Thus I think there is another scenario, at least as plausible as that of 'laying the foundations of subsequent growth'. That is the scenario, first introduced into development economics by Gunnar Myrdal, of cumulative processes and vicious circles leading countries into a poverty trap. The Nigerian case study describes rising unemployment, falling investment, lower real wages, continuing severe debt-servicing problems – all factors which fit better into this second scenario.

In any case, scepticism about our having 'laid the foundations of subsequent growth' does not depend on belief in physical capital investment, Harrod–Domar, ICOR and all that. The picture is no different if we talk about human capital. The proportion of central government expenditure spent on education has fallen from 20.5 per cent to 9.0 per cent in low-income countries; from 17.5 per cent to 13.3 per cent in lower middle-income countries; from 15.4 per cent to 11.0 per cent in Latin America and the Caribbean; and from 15.6 per cent to 10.8 per cent in the severely indebted countries. There are similar declines in health expenditures as a proportion of government expenditure from 5.5 per cent to 2.8 per cent in low-income countries; 5.7 per cent to 4.0 per cent in lower middle-income countries and from 5.9 per cent to 4.4 per cent in the severely indebted countries. Again it will take many years before such a cumulative shortfall can be made up. All this does not look like laying the foundations for growth in terms of the human resource basis.

Third world poverty has increased in absolute numbers although not as a proportion of world population. The current best estimate is that over 1.1 billion people, or 33 per cent of their population, live in poverty; and more than half of them in 'extreme poverty'. Thus more people than ever are exposed to the vicious circles of poverty or 'poverty trap'. The amount of human capital destroyed in the process is incalculable. Part of this may be amenable by market processes and economic 'empowerment' of the poor but not even the most ardent neo-liberal would deny the need for complementary state action to provide opportunities and safety nets for the poor. The World Bank itself, in its 1990 *World Development Report*, with poverty as its main theme, has opened the new decade with an impressive argument for such a 'balanced' or 'double-track' approach, combining labour-intensive growth with social safety nets – back to the Redistribution with Growth strategy of the 1970s? Growth policies are more sustainable if they are simultaneously accompanied by poverty alleviation. Poverty alleviation in turn is more sustainable, or only sustainable, if additional resources are available from domestic growth or external sources. On this at least a genuine consensus could perhaps be emerging. But the study of India, the country with the largest single number of poor, illustrates the obstacles standing in the way of an effective policy of poverty reduction and Nigeria presents an example of increased inequality and poverty.

So there is some reason to be sceptical about the view that the third world economies are now 'leaner and fitter' to face the decade ahead beyond the debt crisis. They are certainly leaner but whether they are fitter remains to be seen. It is probably true in the case of much of Asia, but probably untrue in the case of Africa, Latin America, and the Middle East.

But it seems not very useful to dream in terms of statistical scenarios for a return to paradise lost. Nor is it productive to sit down wearing sackcloth and sprinkling ashes on our heads, wailing about the setbacks and failures of the past. Far better to accept the setbacks of the lost decade as water under the bridge and ask ourselves: Where do we go from here? How can we do better in the future?

Economic projections are notoriously tricky and our record as forecasters is very patchy to say the least. The Nigerian study reminds us how far the country went wrong in forecasting oil prices with very harmful effects on development policies. World Bank projections, whether on commodity prices, growth rates or the results of structural adjustment programmes, have proved chronically over-optimistic and had to be repeatedly revised downward. As a result the World Bank, and all of us, have become more humble about our projections and hedge them with careful assumptions. As Galbraith has said: 'there is nothing wrong with making projections as long as you leave the future out of it'. There is practically no area, from the 'peace dividend', financial flows, the Uruguay Round, oil prices, future technologies, and so on where you could not make plausible optimistic assumptions about the impact on developing countries or equally plausible pessimistic assumptions.

For example, technology may work as much against developing countries as in their favour. It is true that biotechnology, improved health technology, globalization of production due to improved communications technology, and so on may benefit them. But increased replacement of natural raw materials, increased importance of high skills rather than cheap labour, closer integration of R and D with production will operate against them. Nobody can be sure today where the balance will lie. The only thing we can say with confidence is that countries with good technology policies could gain by maximizing the advantages and minimizing the disadvantages, and vice versa. The Indian case study showed the tremendous effect of improved agricultural technology in creating a green revolution, but also its limitations in respect of equitable distribution and poverty reduction.

This last statement can be generalized also for other areas beyond technology. The 1990s could be a decade of great opportunities – especially if we manage to learn from errors of the past – but it also continues one of great dangers lurking for developing countries. The end of the Cold War – assuming that it has finally ended – is a good example: the much-talked-about peace dividend could release new resources for development. Even if it only resulted in an achievement of the theoretically accepted aid level of 0.7 per cent of donor countries' GNP, this would mean an extra $60 billion a year or more and, if the switch out of military expenditures were to increase the growth rate of the OECD countries by only half of one per cent, that, transferred to financing development, would add a further yearly $90 billion (all at 1992 prices). Add to this the resources that could be released by reducing military expenditures within the developing countries themselves – and assuming that all these additional resources were productively invested at reasonable returns – it would not be difficult to construct a hopeful scenario, even a new golden age. On the other hand, the end of the Cold War could equally well lead to a large-scale diversion of resources towards Eastern Europe and the former USSR and the dying away of interest in aid or other forms of development support. That danger of diversion may be strengthened by political factors: the developing countries will no longer be able to manoeuvre for support from West or East in order to 'keep them on our side' or stop them from joining 'the other side'. While up to now the developing countries had to compete 'only' with the USA for the world's limited savings, now they will have to compete not only with the USA – assuming that the US balance of payments deficit will continue – but also with the vast, almost limitless, needs of the former 'second world'.

In fact, as a consequence of the end of the Cold War, we can be fairly certain that the old categories of a first, second and third world will become obsolete in the 1990s. We will still have the first world, the opulent Western industrial OECD countries. We will then have a new second world of less opulent industrial countries in which most of the old second world will be joined by many Asian countries, perhaps including China, but also by Mexico, Chile, Venezuela and others. There will be a reduced Third World which would include the periphery of the former second world and those developing countries which manage a measure of rehabilitation and recovery from the 1980s. Finally there will be a fourth world, increasingly marginalized, of countries (mainly in sub-Saharan Africa) where the vicious circles set in motion by the ravages of the 1980s and of ultra-neo-liberal methods of curing them prove to be too powerful for rehabilitation.

In the light of so many uncertainties, any projections and the assumptions underlying the models on which they are based will reflect the beliefs and wishes of the projectors more than anything else. We are on somewhat safer ground when we turn to the development policies and strategies which are likely to emerge and which may help to cope with such a highly uncertain external environment.

A RETURN TO PRAGMATISM

At the end of Part 1 we had already referred to the somewhat unproductive debate as to whether domestic policies are more or less important than external factors and described this as 'a non-question', and in the case studies of Part 2 we saw the importance of both external and internal factors and of an effective interaction between the two. There is some hope that this debate will recede in the coming decade or at any rate take more productive forms. Good policies are clearly easier to formulate and above all to implement in a favourable economic environment, particularly one associated with capital inflows and agreed debt reduction. The two must go hand in hand; the Bretton Woods institutions in particular need to adopt the more symmetrical approach visualized at Bretton Woods, i.e. to put equal pressure on the powerful and surplus countries which shape the external environment and on the poorer and deficit countries which must improve their policies.

It is hoped that this could be linked with a general return from ideology back to pragmatism. Ideology has dominated both sides of the development debate in the 1980s: on the part of the industrial countries and the institutions which they dominate, this has taken the form of proclaiming not only the dominant importance of so-called good governance but also the detailed prescriptions of what constitutes it. On the part of the developing countries it has taken the form of hammering away at the need for a new international economic order even though in the 1980s this has been done in a less confrontational style against a background of awareness of their weaknesses. A major reform in particular can be hoped for from any such growing consensus on the need for simultaneous and symmetrical action on the external and internal fronts, also demonstrated by our case studies. First of all, the stabilization and structural adjustment agreements under the auspices of the IMF and World Bank which determine the policies of so many developing countries today must be shaped much less on a country-by-country basis and much more within the framework of global commodity markets, global trade expansion, and global debt relief policies.

It is a debatable point whether the presently dominant neo-liberal ideology is bound to shift emphasis away from general economics to specific and diverse characteristics of individual developing countries or not. The basic tenet of the neo-liberal approach is that there are general economic principles, e.g. concerning markets, prices, incentives, and so on which are universal and can be applied to all countries. There is clearly a danger that those with the perceived knowledge of the universally valid economic principles should then fail to modify their application to individual countries sufficiently to take account of their diverse individual circumstances. That indeed is a criticism frequently made in connection with the IMF/World Bank-promoted stabilization and structural adjustment programmes. But this need not necessarily be so. Even if there are universally valid principles, it is still perfectly possible, in their application to individual countries in specific situations, to adapt and modify them to suit different kinds of political, economic, social and administrative realities. It is to the willingness of such adaptation and modification that we must look for the better balance between ideology and pragmatism here suggested. The case studies provide much material for establishing the need for such adaptation and modification. If this is not only theoretically admitted but also practised, in the end the difference between the neo-liberal approach and more structuralist and institutional approaches may turn out to be bridgeable and lead to a real consensus.

A second reform proposal arising from this is that the programmes themselves must be formulated in a much broader negotiating framework than the present largely financial setting. The sectors and interests concerned with the real economy and with different social and economic groups should be much more directly involved. This will also help to make the programmes more country-specific and move them away from their present ideologically-based uniformity. As explained in Part 1, the agreements shaped during the 1980s were at the same time too country-specific (in the sense of blinkered country-by-country negotiations) and yet not country-specific enough (in the sense of being too uniform and giving insufficient consideration to the great variety, indeed uniqueness, of political, economic and social factors in each country). The case studies of Nigeria and India have illustrated this diversity between two important countries.

Quite apart from the end of the Cold War and the potential of the peace dividend, the increasing importance of environmental considerations could be another favourable factor, another silver lining to the generally cloudy outlook for the 1990s. The cooperation of the developing countries is indispensable in protecting the ozone layer, rainforests, endangered species, exhaustible energy resources, and so on of our globe. Even beyond this, there is an increasing realization of the connection between world poverty and environmental deterioration. It is not impossible to visualize that an enlightened new global environmental priority would include poverty alleviation in developing countries as an essential ingredient. The danger here is – once again a cloud to the silver lining – that the richer countries may seek protection of the environment at the expense of the poorer countries – the potential conflicts over logging and agricultural settlement in the rainforest areas are already apparent today. It will be a task for the 1990s to make the environment into an opportunity for world development and to eliminate the inherent risk that it might become an impediment. Opportunities abound, but so also do the risks of such opportunities being lost through policy failure.

Another silver lining with a cloud attached to it is the emerging formation of three major regional blocs among the industrial countries. A North American bloc may well offer great opportunities not just to Mexico but also to other Latin American countries if they can secure better access to North American markets, North American technology, North American capital, and perhaps even North American labour markets. Similarly the East Asian and South-East Asian developing countries could benefit from access to Japanese markets, technology and capital. This creates a special responsibility for the European Community – likely to be further expanded in the course of the decade – to provide similar opportunities for Africa well beyond the present very limited benefits of association.

Where then is the cloud attached to this silver lining? These regional blocs could either be stepping stones towards a free multilateral trading system or they could become 'fortresses', blocking a global multilateral system. It is very much in the interests of developing countries that the former alternative should materialize. Much of this will be decided in the earlier part of the decade, with the GATT Uruguay Round hanging in the balance at the moment of writing. A liberalized multilateral trading system would also provide a better basis than regional blocs for the long-delayed development of South–South trade. Given its present low level, inexplicable on purely economic grounds, there should be considerable upward potential by creating the financial and institutional basis for expanded South–South trade. This is also in the interests of the industrial countries and it should not be beyond the wit of economic statesmanship to find non-confrontational solutions to fill this conspicuous gap in the network of world trade.

A large-scale inflow of capital from the big industrial centres could well help to restore growth and improve the outlook for the 1990s but at the same time carry with it the seeds of a new debt crisis and a new debt trap in the more remote future. Admittedly, the newly incurred debts would not be in the form of fixed commitments but in the form of repatriated profits and dividends. But in its balance of payments impact, and in creating a need for structural adjustment, this new debt problem might not be too dissimilar from the debt crisis of the 1980s.

Part 1 has discussed gaps and distortions in the Bretton Woods system, and Part 2 speaks of the need for 'revitalization of Bretton Woods'. There is also much talk now, in the early years of the 1990s, of a revitalization of the UN. So far this has centred largely, although not exclusively, on the peace-keeping and peace-making responsibilities of the UN, following upon its role in the Gulf War, Namibia, Cambodia, El Salvador and so on. But there is also discussion about an enhanced role in disarmament, protection of the environment, and disaster relief. Furthermore, following upon the UNICEF Report on *Adjustment with a Human Face* and the UNDP Human Resources Development Reports, there is a new emerging paradigm of a division of labour within the UN system between the Bretton Woods institutions and the rest of the UN system. Under this paradigm, anything to do with economics, finance and growth would be within the domain of the IMF and World Bank while the UN would look after human resources, poverty alleviation and social sectors, in addition to the environment and disaster relief. Superficially, this looks like a neat and tidy division which would give the UN a more important role than it has had in the past and which would reflect the comparative advantages of the two types of organization.

Yet it is essentially an untenable and undesirable division. To begin with, it would require that the functions given to the UN should receive the same financial and political support now reserved for the Bretton Woods institutions. Otherwise there would be a danger of the functions allocated to the UN being swept under the table and dying of neglect. Hence, to make this division workable, the UN would have to be given much larger and dependable sources of finance, possibly through new sources of international taxation. Given such a financial strengthening of the UN, the proposed division might be workable, but it is far from clear that this precondition is realized by those advocating the new paradigm.

Second – and perhaps more important – such things as prevention of disasters, as distinct from mere relief, protecting the environment, alleviating poverty, supporting refugees and so on are too much intermixed with economic growth, debt relief, employment creation, and the like to confine these functions to a humanitarian category and divide them from economics and finance.

Finally, this arrangement would leave unsolved the urgent need for better and more democratic macroeconomic global governance. It is clear that the G5 or G7 is neither effective nor democratic and the Bretton Woods institutions are little more than reflections of the G5 or G7 – as evidenced by the distribution of voting power. In the original vision of a new international order after 1945, this function was to be centred in the UN and specifically in its Economic and Social Council, supported by a multilateral soft aid programme administered by the UN. In Part 1 of this book we have described how this initial vision failed to materialize. A true revitalization of the UN would oblige us to look at the UN Charter and the 1945 vision once again. No doubt the world has changed since 1945 and the different elements of this vision would have to be combined in different ways than was then proposed. But in one form or other a more effective and more democratic system of global management is essential, and there seems no candidate in the field other than the UN.

The case studies of Nigeria and India vividly illustrate the difficulties of combining growth and equity objectives. All governments of developing countries – certainly including those of Nigeria and India – as well as those advising them are rhetorically in favour both of growth and of equity and declare their wish and intention to combine them. But in practice this turns out to be extremely difficult. Growth tends to go hand in hand with increased efficiency and increased efficiency often means less employment and less employment means more poverty. Similarly, emphasis on equity and poverty reduction all too often means increased taxation or more inflation or otherwise reduced incentives for the productive sector of the economy and thus may reduce growth. Again it is easy theoretically and on paper to point out ways in which growth and equity could be made to work together: growth could and should be labour-intensive and thus increase employment, and poverty programmes could be of a kind to increase production by providing productive assets and employment for the poor; but once again all this is more easily said than done. Neither Nigeria nor India can be said to have solved this dilemma, although in both countries elements of such a solution can be found.

The equity element in the growth/equity combination encounters the further difficulty of targeting poverty reduction programmes effectively on the intended beneficiaries. Almost by definition, the neediest and most vulnerable groups are also the ones most difficult to reach by public action, especially by public action emanating from a central government. It is here that the question of decentralization to regional and local levels and the involvement of non-governmental organizations and the community itself emerges from the case studies as a problem awaiting progress in the 1990s. This is the principle of 'subsidiarity' now increasingly emphasized in the development discussion.

More generally, although closely related to the problem of growth with equity, there is emerging from the case studies the crucial role of human capital. The decade of the 1990s has opened with the three splendid Human Resources Development Reports of the United Nations Development Programme for 1990, 1991 and 1992. The strengthening of human capital is clearly the long-run answer to the quest for an effective combination of equity and growth. This is not to deny the role of physical investment but its creation as well as its efficiency are increasingly seen as products of human capital formation. For this reason the setbacks during the lost decade of the 1980s in human as well as physical capital formation described earlier in this Part and illustrated in the case studies are particularly worrying. The 'human face', not only for structural adjustment programmes but also for development generally, is not a humanitarian luxury but an economic necessity. It is not least for these reasons that the undue weakness of the UN and its associated agencies and the corresponding undue preponderance of the financial Bretton Woods institutions should be corrected. To create a more balanced and restructured set of international institutions is one of the many tasks facing us in the 1990s and beyond.

General References

References for the works cited in the case studies appear on pp. 108–12 and 155–8.

Bardhan, P. (1984), *The Political Economy of Development in India*, Basil Blackwell, Oxford.

Beckman, B., (1982), 'Whose State? State and capitalist development in Nigeria', *Review of African Political Economy*, No. 23, January–April.

Cooper, Richard N. (1992), *Economic Stabilization and Debt in Developing Countries*, The MIT Press, Cambridge, Massachusetts.

Cornia, A., Jolly, R. and Stewart, F. (eds) (1987), *Adjustment with a Human Face*, A Study by UNICEF, Clarendon Press, Oxford.

Hunt, Diana (1989), *Economic Theories of Development. Analysis of Competing Paradigms*, Harvester Wheatsheaf, UK.

Patel, S. (1985), *India's Regression in the World Economy*, IDS Discussion Paper, August.

Roy, Sumit (1990), *Agriculture and Technology in Developing Countries: India and Nigeria*, Sage Publications, New Delhi/Newbury Park/London.

Sarkar, P. and Singer, H.W. (1991), 'Manufactured Exports of Developing Countries and their Terms of Trade since 1965' in *World Development*, April.

Singer, H.W. (1989), 'Lessons of Post-War Development Experience 1945–1988', *IDS Discussion Paper* No. 260, November.

Singer, H.W. (1991), 'The Uruguay Round of GATT negotiations and Third World trade and development problems', paper delivered in Vienna at a Conference on the GATT negotiations, 28 June.

Smith, Sheila (1982), 'Stories about the world economy: the quest for the grail', Review Article, *Third World Quarterly*, 4 (3), July.

Todaro, Michael P. (1989), *Economic Development in the Third World*, Longman, New York and London.

United Nations (1988), *Handbook of International Trade and Development Statistics*.

Watts, M. (1987), *State, Oil and Agriculture in Nigeria*, Institute of International Studies, University of California, Berkeley, USA.

World Bank (1989), *World Development Report*.

World Bank (1991), *World Development Report*.

Index